The Law of Attraction:

How to Use it to Reach
Your Life's Dreams and Goals...
FAST

Develop
Irresistible
Attraction

Five Easy Steps

Connie Domino, MPH, RN

LOA Quantum Growth, LLC

Raleigh, NC

LOA Quantum Growth, LLC
7805 Tylerton Drive Raleigh, NC 27613
Tel: 919-368-8041
Email: Publisher@LOAQuantum Growth.com

An application to register this book for cataloging has been submitted to the Library of Congress.

First Edition: 2004

Second Edition: 2006

Third Edition: 2007

ISBN: 0-9786158-1-6

ISBN (13) 9-780978-615819

Printed in the United States of America

Cover Design by Candice M. Goble

What people are saying about the LOA Workshop that lead to this book ...

"I increased my sales as a photographer since I have been taking this class from Connie Domino. I just received an unexpected sale of $1,200 for several wedding albums for the parents of the couple, and I just received an event coverage job for $450.00. I was skeptical at first, but now I can see this system really works and works fast just like you said." *Bill S.*

"Connie Domino's workshop has really helped me focus more on the "flow of energy" which is mine to claim. My new business partner and I are opening up a piano studio this summer. I have manifested two free pianos, a space for my studio, free teaching materials, and helpers to paint and repair, etc. Learning how to "get in the energy flow" has allowed me to begin this wonderful business which is my passion with very little expenses up front. This is such a creative period, full of success and 'joy.'" *Joy M.*

"I love Connie Domino's LOA System. It has brought to light things that I have always done but took for granted. Since my first LOA class, I have manifested relationships, several new jobs and a new home." *Donna W.*

"This LOA class is further confirmation in the power of creative thought. We do attract all that we experience. I have manifested a nanny, a summer class and camp schedule, an entertainment center and a forgiveness class." *Julie O.*

"I have manifested financial abundance. I have more sales prospects now than I can handle. I am finding money on the ground almost daily. I have doubled my income since last year." *Chris O.*

"After taking Connie's workshop, I have far exceeded my target to grow my wellness business including gathering customers and new business partners. My business has extended into three new states and my check has increased every month since the workshop -- sometimes with double digit growth. I am amazed at how simple it was to follow Connie's system and grow my business." *Rosemary M.*

"Connie Domino has opened me up to awareness of synchronicity in my life. My desire was a relationship. I have manifested an opportunity to spend a week with a man that I met four years ago at a time that I wasn't open to a relationship. After I wrote my affirmation for a relationship, this man reentered my life unexpectedly." *AR*

"I got exactly what I have been affirming. I started work two weeks ago for a wonderful company. I have two of the most qualified managers that I could ask for. I got exactly the amount of money that I affirmed." *Johanna S.*

"Connie Domino has brought to light the powers we all possess to bring greater prosperity and happiness into our lives. I personally have manifested a greater sense of well-being and greater prosperity through my harp performance business. I have booked additional performances and plan to add a website." *Mary B.*

To my wonderful husband, Mike,

and my beautiful children, Joanna and Matthew,

who support my dreams and goals day in and day out.

Henry David Thoreau[1]

"If one advances confidently in the direction of his dreams, and endeavors to live the life which he had imagined, he will meet with a success unexpected in common hours. He will put some things behind, will pass an invisible boundary, new universal and more liberal laws will begin to establish themselves around and within him, or the old laws be expanded, and interpreted in his favor in a more liberal sense, and he will live with the license of a higher order of beings."

Acknowledgments

To my tremendous Mama and Daddy, who told me "I could be anything I set my heart and mind to," and are some of my best LOA students.

To Jeff and Donna, for their suggestions and input (especially Jeff's input on the visualization section) and for editing the first draft of my book.

To John, who noticed I was "really on to something," and introduced me to Katharine and Ron.

To Katharine and Ron, who have believed in me since the day we met.

To all my inspirational LOA students, who have taken this most amazing journey with me these last five years, and have been my teachers.

To God and all Your Divine Helpers, whose guidance I feel continuously.

Orah [2]

"Energy is the essence of life. Every day you decide how you're going to use it by knowing what you want and what it takes to reach that goal, and by maintaining focus."

TABLE OF CONTENTS

PART II – Five Easy Steps to Getting What You Desire FAST!

**PART III - Tools, Strategies, and Techniques for
Assisting Your Desired Goals to Manifest Even Faster!**

Preface

I was sitting in a Botany class in my second year of college when I was first introduced to the concept of "human potential" and "positive mental attitude." It was the late 1970's, and I was 18 years old. I found it curious that a Botany professor would think it necessary to teach his students about positive mental attitude. Between taking tests that included walking through the woods naming flowering plants and trees, we were instructed to read and complete a book report on *The Power of Positive Thinking* by Norman Vincent Peale. We were also instructed to check out tapes by a man with a deep, sleepy voice named Earl Nightingale and listen to them through big headphones in the library.

My professor, who appeared to be in his early 50s, told us that these seemingly strange homework assignments were important to teach, even in a Botany class, because they could help determine the course of our lives. In my young mind, I considered that assigning unusual homework might have been his way of celebrating some kind of mid-life crisis. I knew from my psychology professor that a man named Eric Erickson had said that people in their 40's and 50's reach a stage where they must experience generativity or they will become stagnated. Generativity means that people must engage in something that has meaning to them, something that is creative, something that makes a difference to others. I wasn't sure what "stagnated" looked like, but it didn't sound like a fun place to be. I figured the least I could do was help this poor aging professor avoid reaching the awful state of "stagnation" by going along with his crusade. I also figured it could help me get the "A" in Botany.

There was only one problem … I wasn't really into reading books back then. My parents had never read many books, and it just seemed reading took too much time and energy to be bothered with. So, to complete a book report, I would only read the introduction, the conclusion and the back cover. I was bright enough to pull it off, and soon received a good grade on my book report about *The Power of Positive Thinking*. Imagining I was clever in getting away with writing another book report on a book I didn't actually read, I didn't realize that my Botany

16

Develop Irresistible Attraction

professor had planted a seed in my mind that wouldn't take root until years later. He was absolutely correct when he said, "the power of positive thinking can determine the course of our lives."

It would be years later before I was reintroduced to the concept of "positive mental attitude." It was now the mid-1980's, and many books had been written by people talking about how a positive mental attitude (commonly referred to as PMA) could make a person rich. I had married by this time, and my husband was involved in a business that required its associates to read PMA books. These books were supposed to be "magic" in turning us from just regular folks striving to make a living into some kind of "money making magnets." I was taught that PMA could not only "change the course of my life," it could "make me rich too."

With all this in mind, I decided that I had better read more than just the introduction, conclusion, and back cover of PMA books to find out what all the "hoopla" was really about. My husband brought home books with titles like: *How to Have Confidence and Power in Dealing with People, The Secret of Success, See You At the Top, and How to Start a Conversation and Make Friends*. These books were by people with last names like Giblin, Allen, Ziglar, and Gabor, respectively. However, the books that interested me the most had titles with the word "think" in them because I had always loved to think. They had titles like *You Are What You Think* and *Think and Grow Rich,* by authors Hooper and Hill, respectively.

It was then I learned the concept that it's not just what you "think," but it's also "what you say to yourself" all while you're "thinking." The books *What to Say When You Talk To Yourself* and *The Self-talk Solution* by Shad Helmstetter really intrigued me at this point. Now I understood! You had to think rich thoughts, say positive things about yourself to yourself, all while hanging out with positive people who were also thinking rich thoughts and saying positive things. It seemed simple enough.

One of the things that I learned after attending numerous PMA workshops and seminars is that 90 percent of Americans never write down their goals. In fact, most Americans spend more time planning their summer vacation than planning their life's direction and goals! I was told by many of the workshop

Preface

leaders that I should develop a 2-to 5-year plan for my goals and dreams, and a 10-year plan for lifelong dreams. Then, after writing down these plans for the future, I should dream build, visualize my dream, meditate on my dream, and place pictures of my dream on the refrigerator.

By this time, I was very busy thinking, talking to myself, visualizing, dream building, meditating, hanging out with positive people, reading positive books and listening to positive tapes. The only problem was that I wasn't getting richer. In fact, I was actually getting poorer because I was spending all my extra money on positive workshops, positive tapes, positive books, positive meetings, and positive dream building, as well as purchasing positive products from my husband's business. Don't worry about getting poorer, I was told, because you have both a 2 to 5-year plan and a 10-year plan and something was bound to happen after years of all this positive activity.

So after 4 years of "extreme positive activity," my husband and I were exhausted. We had our first baby, a beautiful daughter in 1989, and wondered when we would ever sleep again. All the money spent on PMA was now needed for child rearing. We had become somewhat disillusioned with the PMA movement because after working our 2-to 5-year plan, we hadn't become rich at all. Instead, we were in debt.

However, we knew there was an element that made PMA work for some people, because there were plenty of successful people who used the PMA principles. I began to think about and study these people as I wanted to figure out what made them different from those of us for whom the PMA principles didn't work. Were they more outgoing, more friendly, more intelligent, or just more lucky? We even considered they might be "shysters," and the rest of us were just "suckers" with a big letter "S" emblazoned on our foreheads invisible to everyone but shysters. However, they didn't look any different than the rest of us. They were excited and enthusiastic, but didn't seem smarter than we were. What was the key element? What was the difference? What was the trick, the key that made PMA work? Why did it work for some and not for others? It would be an entire decade before I discovered the answer to this very important question.

Throughout the 1990's, I began to read PMA books that had a big spiritual component. These books taught me principles that resonated as truth in my mind. By the mid-1990's, my daughter was having trouble with reading, writing and math in the local public school where we had placed her. I was pregnant with my son and working full-time. The testing, tutoring and private school where my husband and I placed our daughter just added to our mounting debt load. To make matters worse, after my son was born, I developed a hardy case of the "baby blues" for which I sought professional assistance. It was then that the spiritual counselor I had found gave me a book to read that changed my life - *The Dynamic Laws of Prosperity* by Catherine Ponder. The book was not only positive, but it also contained a strong spiritual element, which had been the missing link for me in the PMA movement. For the first time in my life, I read that we are powerful spiritual beings having an Earthly experience. That really excited me!

In the year 2000 one of my ministers, Jack Graff, introduced me to the book entitled *Excuse Me Your Life is Waiting,* by Lynn Grabhorn. This book was a perfect compliment to the *Dynamic Laws of Prosperity.* Not only did Lynn focus on the principle that your thoughts create your reality, but she added that your thoughts can lead to feelings that can lead to a vibrational energy level that can manifest your destiny.

To the concept of "thinking" I now added "feeling" and "vibrating energy." With the principles outlined in these two books combined with the many other positive spiritual books I had read by this time, I developed the "Irresistible Attraction Workshop" based on the *Law of Attraction.*

In September 2001, I joined forces with my friend Cheri to teach the Irresistible Attraction class at our Church. We had 10 people in our first class, and designed it to run for four weeks with each class being about two hours in length. We had met two times when the attack on the World Trade Center occurred on September 11, 2001. Only two people came back the week after the attack. The good news was that both of them had manifested the major goals they had been working on for several years!

The first woman had been trying to establish a dating life for a year and a-half with no success. That week, she told us that four men had called her. The other woman had been trying to remodel her house for over two years. During the workshop

Preface

she told us that one of her beauty shop clients had visited her house that very week. Her client's husband told her that he could remodel her house for $200 instead of the $5000 that she had thought it would cost. I was absolutely amazed at how quickly these women had met their goals because both had been actively working on them for some time.

Although I was greatly intrigued, I knew I would need to repeat the workshop to ensure these fast results were not just a "fluke" of some kind. In January of 2002, I repeated the class as the only facilitator with twenty people in attendance. Again, people began to have very quick results in meeting their life's goals – some in as little as one to two class sessions.

Since this time, I have repeated the *Develop Irresistible Attraction -- Law of Attraction* (LOA) workshop many times, both locally and nationally, for agencies, organizations and churches. In addition, people from all over the country and world have attended my LOA workshops for building a business called *Business Abundance for the Entrepreneur.* The results became more and more fast and amazing. Workshop participants experienced: more money, new romantic relationships, new jobs, job promotions, a boost in sales, better family relationships, a new career direction, improved health, more peace, harmony and clarity -- many after only one to two class sessions! One school volunteer even manifested a newly built building for a charter school for underprivileged children in only six months.

I have written this book to share with you this amazing, fast technique for obtaining your life's dreams and goals. I have seen so many people incredibly happy and transformed by the LOA method that I will do whatever is necessary to support you in obtaining your goals and dreams -- fast.

Blessings Galore,
Connie Domino
April 2007

Develop Irresistible Attraction

Napoleon Hill [1]

Whatever the mind of a man [or woman] can Conceive and Believe it can Achieve.

PART I

Everything You Need to Know to Activate *the Law of Attraction*

Patrice Vecchione[2]

"Belief in ability rekindles your spiritual nature. It implies confidence in what is yet to come, what is unseen and unapparent. If you stake belief in what is beyond you, … you can draw from that which is greater than the solitary self to do your work."

CHAPTER 1
Introduction

Who Will Benefit Most From This Book?

This book was written for those who are serious about making their dreams, goals and desires manifest quickly. Within its pages is an easy five-step program that will teach you a simple formula that you can use again and again to make your grandest dreams come true -- fast!!

Many of the ideas presented here are not new. You will recognize them, as they are contained in many of today's most popular self-help, positive spiritual and mental attitude books. What I discovered, through many years of reading these books is that although they covered many of the principles and laws that I will cover in this book, they didn't place them in a simple, practical formula within a context (the popular framework of goal setting) that people were familiar with and accustomed to using.

I also found that almost all of the goal setting books ever written would instruct readers to set their goals, but would never ask readers how they "felt" about the goals they set. I discovered that a person's underlying thoughts and feelings about the goals they set, or the vehicle through which they were choosing to meet their goals (if those feelings were negative) could act as "energy blocks" or "psychological blocks" to keep the goal from manifesting. I found that people didn't always recognize their underlying feelings and thoughts about a desired goal. I soon discovered a quick way to assist people in recognizing these underlying feelings and thoughts was to assist them with examining their self-talk and how it evolved from childhood.

When I combined all these discoveries together, I produced a simple five-step formula that will assist people to become extremely clear about their desired goals. In addition, this formula will assist them, through understanding their self-talk, **to identify,** and through the process of positive affirmations, **to remove** any underlying negative thoughts and feelings about their goals.

When energetic or psychological blocks around a desired goal are removed, the goal will manifest very quickly. Most other positive self-help and goal setting books tell you the "What." This book teaches you the "How" in the simplest step-by-step formula I have ever seen.

One of the most important things I discovered in developing this process is that it is not enough for an author of positive self-help books to present good ideas for their readers to follow; they must present those ideas in a familiar (easy to understand and implement) framework. This way the reader can easily incorporate the ideas into their everyday life and achieve quick results. The design of the framework, template, or paradigm through which these life-changing concepts are presented, must itself account for all of the complex psychological, sociological and theological concepts that make it work. In other words, the goal setting template (the steps to follow) must boil down all the theories that go into its making so that any user at any level of sophistication can achieve quick – almost miraculous appearing – results without ever needing to understand the dynamics of what makes the matrix work, unless of course they choose to. In fact, the framework must be so user-friendly, so easy to use, and so understandable as to almost be what my college Western Civilization professor used to call, "village idiot proof." An analogy is that you don't have to know everything about how a TV works to plug in it, turn it on and watch your favorite show.

I am thrilled to be able to share with you this simple five-step goal setting process. It requires only 4 written exercises and has been anecdotally proven by hundreds of my Law of Attraction (LOA) students. This system has assisted them in achieving their desires, dreams and goals so fast, it made their heads spin. It can do the same for you! So, strap on your seatbelt and get ready for the exciting journey. You'll just love it!!!!

Introduction

What Is the *Law of Attraction* (LOA)?

"Someday, after mastering the winds, the waves, the tides and gravity, we shall harness for God the energies of Love, and then, for the second time in the history of the world, man will discover fire." -- Pierre Teilhard De Chardin [3]

The *Law of Attraction* is a universal law open to use by anyone that understands it. Just like the law of gravity, it is universal and unchanging. Remember Isaac Newton getting hit on the head by the apple? Remember Galileo dropping light and heavy objects off the Leaning Tower of Pisa to see which one would land first? These scientists were researching and discovering the law of gravity. They discovered that "gravity" is what makes an apple fall from a tree instead of float. It affects the ocean tides, and literally holds our bodies to the Earth, so we can walk or ride in our cars without floating away. The law of gravity is eternal and unchanging. Scientists didn't invent it, they only named it, learned about its properties, and learned how to utilize it. When your doctor instructs you to place a swollen limb on a pillow, you are being taught to use the law of gravity to reduce your swelling. Once we came to understand the law of gravity, we began to use it more and more.

While the law of gravity is a physical law that has influence over our physical existence, the *Law of Attraction* is a *spiritual* or *social* law. Spiritual laws can be used to affect the physical or material world. We are only now beginning to understand the properties of the *Law of Attraction*. However, as we continue to grow in our knowledge and understanding of its properties, we will be able to use it more and more … just like the law of gravity.

Both of these "laws" involve an exchange of energy. When an apple disconnects from its limb, it is pulled to the ground by gravity. The falling to the ground involves motion and a transfer of energy. Energy is ever-present, all around us, and literally what we are made of, body and soul. I like to call it "universal energy" or "God energy." The important thing is to not get caught up in the semantics, but to understand that everything is composed of energy, and that energy travels in waves. Scientists have discovered that energy is neither created nor destroyed, but changes from one state to another (this is known in physics as the 1st Law of Thermodynamics). Therefore, energy is malleable. For the purpose of our discussion, you can think of energy as "Play dough." In that sense, the energy stuff of the universe can be fashioned by our creative process to make our dreams come true. At this point, you may be saying that this sounds way "too goofy" to be true, but hang on and I will teach you the most exciting tools I have ever discovered for making your desires manifest quickly.

So how does the *Law of Attraction* affect you personally?

The *Law of Attraction* teaches us that:

♦ All that we are experiencing in our lives, we have attracted (both the good and bad) by our thoughts, feelings, prayers, actions, inactions, and soul level decisions.

♦ We can change our circumstances by changing the way we think (and *feel*), what we believe, what we say to ourselves (our self-talk), and the actions we take.

♦ The Energy needed to make our dreams come true is already provided, already available in existence, and is waiting for our thoughts and beliefs to manifest it into the material world.

♦ Love is the Energy, Belief is the Vehicle for Manifestation. There is nothing in existence stronger than Love and Belief.

We can literally create our reality, create the life we want, and manifest our desires, goals and dreams by using the *Law of Attraction*. By following the process I will teach, you will learn 5 easy steps to manifest what you desire quickly.

Semantics

> *"I believe the very purpose of our life is to seek happiness. That's clear. Whether we believe in a religion or not, whether one believes in this religion or that religion, we are all seeking something better in life. So, I think the very motion of our life is towards happiness."* - The Dalai Lama [4]

At this point, it is important for me to discuss the meaning of words used in the LOA process. From the "get go," humans have been developing symbols and language to communicate their ideas and needs. Different symbols, and even different dialects and languages, were developed for the same word. For example, there are many words and expressions for greeting a person in the English language including: "hi," "hello," "hey," "how are you," "what's up," "greetings," and "salutations," to name a few. Other languages also have their words for saying hello. The point is, there are different words and expressions that all mean the same thing.

The same principle can be applied to universal laws. It really doesn't matter what you call them or which language you use, they all work the same way. For example, you can call gravity: a force, gravitation, a pull towards the center of the Earth, heaviness or weight, and it still means the same thing, acts in the same way and has the same set of properties. Our preferred semantics are for our own understanding and clarity as they do not change the properties of the object or law being referred to.

It is important to discuss semantics when teaching about the *Law of Attraction* because it is one of the universe's spiritual or social laws. People have a range of different words and expressions they use to describe their understanding of anything spiritual. In fact, this is precisely why I explain to my LOA students that if I use a word to describe a spiritual idea, concept, or being that isn't the word they prefer or use, they should simply replace my word with their preferred word in their head. I would instruct you as the reader to do the very same thing. Like the law of gravity, the *Law of Attraction* works the same no matter what words we prefer to use in describing it. For example, I may use the words: energy, God's energy, or universal energy, interchangeably. I was raised in the Christian tradition, so I am most familiar with the teachings of Jesus and will use some of his examples. However, all major religions include examples and you may wish to choose an example from the faith tradition and teachings you are most familiar and comfortable with. LOA works equally well for those with no particular faith tradition.

The main thing is to provide your own words and interpretations where needed, and don't get caught up in the "semantics," or you will miss one of the most exciting opportunities for personal growth I have ever discovered.

> *"By the end of the 1970s, we were intuiting a new awareness, a new sense of self, and a higher flow of experience that would replace the old habits and reactions that plagued us. The fuller life we sensed was not about mere psychological growth. The new awareness necessitated a deeper transformation that could only be called spiritual."* -- James Redfield[5]

The Power of Thought

> *"Let a man radically alter his thoughts, and he will be astonished at the rapid transformation it will effect in the material conditions of his life."* - James Allen [6]

Researchers have been studying the power of thought for some time. The most interesting and famous studies have focused on "healing thought, directed prayer or meditation." Larry Dossey, MD, describes in his book *Healing Words* the study of prayer conducted by Cardiologist Randolph Byrd in a coronary care unit at San Francisco General Hospital.[7] The study was scientifically designed according to very strict criteria. It was a randomized, double blind study with a control group, which means neither the patients, nurses, or doctors, knew which group the patients were assigned to. Over a ten month time period, a computer randomly assigned 192 patients to the treatment group (meaning those patients being prayed for) and 201 patients to the control group (those patients who were not remembered in prayer). Various religious groups were recruited to pray for patients in the treatment group. Patients had between 5 and 7 people praying for them. The people praying were only given the patient's first name, and a brief description of their diagnosis and condition. They were then instructed to pray each day, but were not instructed how to pray.

The research results demonstrated that the treatment group of coronary patients who were prayed for differed from the control group, who were not prayed for, in the following areas:

◆ Those in the treatment group were less likely to require antibiotics for postoperative infections, when compared with the control group.

◆ Those in the treatment group were less likely to develop pulmonary edema (fluid in their lungs) with only 6 in the treatment group, compared with 18 in the control group.

◆ None in the treatment group required assistance with breathing by being intubated (an artificial airway tube placed in the trachea) and connected to a ventilator (mechanical breathing machine), while 12 in the control group required mechanical ventilation.

◆ Fewer patients in the treatment group died, although not enough to be considered statistically significant.

Dossey reflected on this study by saying, "If the technique being studied had been a new drug or a surgical procedure instead of prayer, it would almost certainly have been heralded as some sort of 'breakthrough.'" Critics of the study note that certain areas were not controlled for, such as the denomination of the people praying, the experience of the doctors caring for the patient, the skill of the people praying, any outside prayer for those in the treatment or control group, and differences in the patient's "coping style" with being in the coronary care unit. Any area not carefully controlled for can possibly influence the results of a research study. However, Dossey mentions that Dr. William Nolan, who has written a book debunking faith healing, acknowledged that this study will "stand up to scrutiny" and maybe doctors ought to be writing on their order sheets "Pray three times a day. If it works, it works."

30

Develop Irresistible Attraction

Research has also been conducted studying the power of focused thought, meditation and/or prayer on nonhuman subjects like yeast, mold and bacteria. Scientists wanted to know if thought traveled in waves like electromagnetic radiation, such as X-rays, TV waves, radio waves, microwaves, etc. They also wanted to know if thoughts would deteriorate at a distance like ultraviolet rays.

Dr. Dossey also describes research studies that have been conducted on bacteria, fungi and even cancer cells. To set up their experiment, scientists placed Petri dishes of bacteria or fungi in a lab. Then they placed the people who would use the power of their thoughts to affect the bacteria or fungi at varying distances from the lab. They told the people to concentrate on the bacteria or fungi in the first set of Petri dishes thinking of them increasing, and the second set of Petri dishes, thinking of the bacteria or fungi decreasing. The scientists also had a set of Petri dishes set over to the side that would be the control group. The control group would not be concentrated on at all. The scientists discovered that the Petri dishes for which the people concentrated on the bacteria or fungi growing, did exactly that to a significant degree. The Petri dishes where the people concentrated on the bacteria or fungi decreasing, did exactly that to a significant degree. The Petri dishes in the control group, which were not focused on, did not change significantly.

Next, the scientists wanted to know if the thoughts the people used to affect the bacteria or fungi traveled in waves that deteriorated at a distance. They separated the people from the bacteria by varying distances and found the same results happened at a significant distance as when the people were in the same building with the bacteria.

Increasingly, scientific research is being conducted on the power of thought, meditation, and prayer, proving what many people have known anecdotally for years — that the mind is a powerful instrument.

(The above section adapted from Larry Dossey's book *Healing Words*) [8]

Introduction

How to Get the Most From This Book

"I think the things that impressed me the most were the simplicity of his thinking and his faith in the ability of the human mind to understand the workings of nature. Throughout his life, Einstein believed that human reason was capable of leading to theories that would provide correct descriptions of physical phenomena. In building a theory, his approach had something in common with that of an artist; he would aim for simplicity and beauty (and beauty for him was, after all, essentially simplicity)." -- Professor Nathan Rosen, Albert Einstein's assistant [9]

I can't tell you how many times I have bought books that contained exercises for me to complete, and I would just read right over the exercises and keep going. In retrospect, one of the main reasons I didn't complete the exercises is there were just too many. Too many exercises, too many steps, and too many days, weeks, months, years before I could expect my desired goal to manifest. In fact, the last two books I picked up each had 15 different steps to plow through before you reached any kind of success. Each step had several different exercises I needed to actively engage in just to complete that one step.

I don't know about you, but I want a method that is simple, quick and understandable. When I cook for my busy family, I have the most success with recipes that have no more than three to five ingredients. When I was growing up, I was never a person that could collect all those cereal box tops from specially marked packages, fill out the form, find a mailing envelope, address the envelope, find a stamp, get to the post office and mail the box tops in hopes to receive my small surprise toy, that I could expect to be delivered in four to six weeks.

This was just too many hoops to jump through! I wanted the surprise toy to come in the box of cereal I picked off the shelf, and sometimes it did.

This is precisely why I have narrowed the LOA process down into five easy steps, with just four written exercises. I figured if I had the time and willingness to complete only four written exercises in just five steps, so could most people.

Develop Irresistible Attraction

The written exercises will be presented with an explanation and directions for completing them. Then, we'll talk about some of the typical answers I've gotten from people who have attended my LOA workshops. With the exercises, we will mainly focus on the technique of completing the forms. The format itself will actually assist with expediting your manifestations making it important for you to fill out each of the forms completely.

After the first three written exercises, we will look at sensorializing your goals, or how to make them real to your five or more senses. I have found that when working with the *Law of Attraction*, it is very helpful to not only *think* about what you desire, but to get in touch with the *feelings* associated with having and experiencing your desires. We will also look at two major techniques or laws of the universe available for you to use to manifest your goals quickly – The *Law of Creating a Vacuum* and the *Law of Forgiveness*. Then, I have provided some detailed instructions for completing your Plan of Action for each of the three desired goals you have written.

After all four written exercises, we will look at examples of how to get energy moving and then "stay in the flow" to expedite the manifestation of your desired goals. We will also examine the four areas where my LOA students most often set their goals. Lastly, but not least, we will look at some of the tremendous success stories of people who have taken the class.

CHAPTER 2
Looking Back to Move Forward

Before we can move forward, we must look back. It is absolutely essential that we take a look at the people who first shaped our values, our self-talk, and in large part our self-image. Once we have looked back, then we will discover how our current self-talk may be either holding us back, or moving us forward toward making our desires manifest.

These first two exercises involve looking back. It's good to look back over our life to discover if anything said or done has influenced where we're at now. Sometimes things said in our childhood no longer apply to us as adults. We need to recognize what those things were, so we can choose to let them go.

The first written exercise is called the "Inventory of Influence for Values." The purpose of this exercise is to determine who or what first shaped our values in life. It is important to determine this because we will find that these people, to this day, can affect our self-talk. We will discover that in large part, it is our self-talk and feelings associated with this talk that shape our current reality. Keep in mind that the people or things that have shaped your values may have changed over the course of time. It is fine to specify "as a child" or "as an adult" by an item, if necessary. You can also have more than one "number one" influence.

Please fully complete this exercise with a pencil or pen before moving to the next exercise.

Develop Irresistible Attraction

REMEMBER!

The four exercises complete a formula or a recipe that activates the Law of Attraction to work for you. You must complete each exercise by fully filling out the form associated with the exercise.

Key Exercise Number 1 – Inventory of Influence for Our Values

Listed below are some possible sources of influence: persons and methods that helped us form our ideas and values. Place an "X" next to those that had no influence and do not apply. Then rank the items, with the most influential ranked "1," the next influential ranked "2," continuing to the least influential. It's perfectly OK to have more than one item ranked the same; for example you may have the influence of your mother and father equally ranked.

_____ your father

_____ your mother

_____ your brother(s)

_____ your sister(s)

_____ your children

_____ your grandparent(s)

_____ your aunt(s)

_____ your uncle(s)

_____ your cousin(s)

_____ your health practitioner

_____ your adult friends

_____ school/educational classes/teachers

_____ your significant other

_____ educational reading

_____ entertaining reading

_____ movies/television/music

_____ your own experiences

_____ your church or other religious organization

_____ other (explain) _____

Processing the "Inventory of Influence for Our Values" Exercise

What did you learn from this exercise? Did the people and things that shaped your values as a child (and now as an adult) change over the course of time? If so, why? Are your values still very similar to those of your parents and/or the people who raised you as a child?

Most of my class participants list their "mother" as the number one influence in shaping their values in life. "Good ole Mom" still ranks supreme in this category. The second number one influence is their "father." "Dear ole Dad" didn't get left out, for sure. Then, grandparents, siblings, aunts and uncles generally get the next highest ratings in that order.

Other items that make the top three most important influence of values include: "my own experiences," "my significant other," school and Church or religious organizations.

It's interesting to note that in our media-saturated culture, movies/television/music rarely get ranked in forming life values.

36

Develop Irresistible Attraction

The Inventory of Influence for Life's Values exercise leads right into our next written exercise. So, keep that pen or pencil handy, and let's get started. In the self-talk exercise we will be examining what those people who most influenced our values (the people who raised us) told us about ourselves, both positive and negative. Then, we will look at our own self-talk and what we tell ourselves about ourselves, both positive and negative. Some participants even add a third category about what their significant other has told them - both positive and negative.

Key Exercise Number 2 – Self-Talk: Looking Back to Move Forward

List 3 Positive Things Your Parents/Guardians Told You About Yourself.

(If you can't think of 3 items, list at least 1 or 2)

1. _____

2. _____

3. _____

List 3 Negative Things Your Parents/Guardians Told You About Yourself.

1. _____

2. _____

3. _____

Looking Back To Move Forward

List 3 Positive Things You Say About Yourself To Yourself And/Or Others.

1. _____

2. _____

3. _____

List 3 Negative Things You Say About Yourself To Yourself And/Or Others.

1. _____

2. _____

3. _____

Processing the "Self-Talk" Exercise

"As a child, I learned that spontaneous outbursts of truth about big people, instinctual perceptions about wrong doings by big people, and clearly observed acts of hypocrisy committed by big people were not to be discussed, or challenged. I would do all in my power to honor the feelings and desires of these people, even when it meant dishonoring myself." -- Iyanla Vanzant [1]

Some participants in my LOA workshops really have an "ah-ha" moment during this exercise. There are always about three or four people out of 30 – 50 that cannot remember one thing their parents/guardians ever said to them, either positive or negative, about themselves. A slightly larger number of about six to seven people can remember plenty of negative things their parents or guardians said to them growing up, but no positive things. A very few participants, usually one to two, can only remember positive things their parents said to them about themselves. The large majority of the group remembers both positive and negative things their parents/guardians said to them about themselves.

Interestingly enough, a significant number of people have contradictory things listed. For example, their parents would say they were "smart," which was positive, and turn around and say they were "dumb." One man's mom was very positive on the one hand, and would say, "Life is just a bowl full of cherries." Then, she would also say, "be careful, it's not safe out there." As a result, this man felt it was difficult for him to manifest success in his career and relationships in that he always had the feeling that "something's not quite safe about this."

I also found that many people have strong parental scripts that still play in their heads and have formed their current reality. The parental script I hear most often is "You must work hard for a living." When I would ask the participants who had that script, "And do you work hard for a living?" they would answer, "Yes, very hard." It had actually never occurred to them that a person could work in the area of their talent and passion, in a line of work they absolutely loved, make plenty of money, and it would not seem like work at all, and certainly wouldn't feel "hard."

Another interesting (but not surprising) finding is their own self-talk usually matched that of their parents or guardians in one way or another. If their parents told them they were fat, they would have as their self-talk, "I am fat." If their parents told them they were "too skinny," they would still feel "skinny," even if their body didn't look "skinny" anymore. Their body image had become fixed in their mind early on.

Also, the areas of life where they had experienced success were usually the areas of life where their parents had given them positive feedback. Those folks whose parents told them they were "smart" usually had no problem manifesting higher education and/or profitable careers. However if their parents had told the same people they were "hard to get along with," they would have a more difficult time manifesting satisfying relationships. Participants whose parents had told them they were "compassionate and friendly," would often say about themselves, "I am a good friend," or a "good parent." However, just as many people who experienced a bad childhood, would have in their own self-talk that they were a "good parent." They became determined to have a better relationship with their own children.

Just as in the last example above, for some participants negative things that parents had said would actually end up being a person's strength. For example, one woman had listed under negatives that her parents had told her she was "stubborn," However, under her positive self-talk list, she had written down that she was a person who "always got things done." It would seem to me that a little stubbornness might go a long way in developing a person who "always got things done." Many people listed under negatives that their parents said they were quite "busy, spirited, hyperactive." These people would also many times turn into adults who were quite "creative and positively productive."

> *"I ran across a teacher a number of years ago who made something astonishingly clear to me. She said, 'consider the possibility that your biggest faults are your grandest assets, simply with the volume turned up just a tiny bit too high.'"*-- Neale Donald Walsch [2]

When I turned forty, I discovered that I still had what our society would call "issues." My issues didn't go away through four decades of living. However, when the LOA process helped me become clear about my life's purpose, I was able to make peace with my issues. I found that what others had earlier called my issues — "being loud, opinionated, rebellious of the status quo, the absentminded professor, loving an audience," actually became the strengths that I needed to carry forth with my life's calling.

Again, the purpose of this exercise was to look back at what your parents told you about yourself and your current self-talk about yourself. Positive self-talk can actually manifest positive desires into our lives, while negative self-talk can create energy blocks or what we call "boulders" that can actually block a manifestation from coming true.

Also, it is important to note any feelings that came up for you during this exercise. It can be very emotional for some people to examine the past. Just note your feelings, don't judge them. Simply be with them.

An Optional, but Powerful Exercise – Turning the Negative Things That Were Said to You into Affirmations

"If during childhood, an aspect of your basic self was repeatedly criticized, or distrusted, and you came to believe you were insufficient or too demanding or a wisecracker, the inner self was wounded. That wound tends to get carried into adulthood and may manifest as self doubt." -- Patrice Vecchione[3]

When you are ready, you may choose to take the negative things that your parents said (from your self-talk Exercise Number 2 on page 36) and turn them into positive "affirmations." Visualize your parents saying these opposite, positive things to you as a child and adult. You may choose to visualize them hugging you and feel the warmth between you. You don't have to complete this exercise until you are ready. If you are not ready at this time in your life, it's perfectly fine to wait until you are. This optional exercise can be emotional and powerfully healing, so being ready for it is very important. You may choose to turn your negative self-talk into positive affirmative statements as well. You can say them to yourself and even give yourself hugs and pats on the back.

An example would be if your parents told you that you are "dumb, lazy and just don't try hard enough." Your affirmation would be to picture in your mind (or hear in your mind) your parents saying, "you are smart, productive, and beautiful and we love you and cherish you just the way you are." Whatever they told you, flip it around into its positive, write it down and say it to yourself picturing your parents looking into your eyes, giving you a hug or both.

Looking Back To Move Forward

This leads us to Key Exercise Number 3 (see page 101) where we will write down our major life desires as positive affirmations. But first, we will need some direction about how to write our goals as affirmations.

Develop Irresistible Attraction

Oprah [1]

"If you want your life to be more rewarding, you have to change the way you think."

CHAPTER 3
Self-Talk and Affirmations

How to Develop Specific, Measurable, Behavioral, Positive Affirmations

"Self-talk prescribes our self-esteem. With our self-talk, we plant in our unconscious what will grow in our lives. We either encourage or discourage ourselves; we lift ourselves up or put ourselves down. The quality of self-talk determines whether we are our own best friend or worst enemy. Only when we turn in and listen to the old messages from the past can we begin to free ourselves of their grip on our present life." -- Dr. Louise Hart [2]

Again, self-talk is so important because you can create your reality by the things you say to yourself. Some researchers say that your brain only hears positive statements and doesn't hear words like "no" and "don't." When I make the statement "don't eat ice cream," your brain hears "eat ice cream." For example: "Don't eat a delicious, chocolate-drenched, smooth and creamy ice cream sundae." What did you hear, feel, visualize or think when I made that statement? Read it again, more slowly, and process what happens. Even though I used the word "don't," most people actually see or taste that sundae. Some people even salivate and their stomachs growl. In fact, whenever my editor reads this section of the book, she just has to go out and buy an ice cream sundae to eat. Like I said, words are powerful.

You can begin by leaving the word "don't" out of your talk to both yourself and others, especially children. Tell children what you "desire them to do," instead of what you "don't" want them to do. Instead of saying "Johnnie, don't leave your shoes on the carpet," say, "Johnnie, put your shoes upstairs in your room, please." The subconscious mind takes statements and thoughts literally and will manifest for you the information you give it in your body and your life.

Develop Irresistible Attraction

"Positive internal dialogue allows you to know your history, yet move beyond it. It allows you to 'rise above your raising.'" -- Phillip C. McGraw, PhD. "Dr. Phil"[3]

The first step to understanding your self-talk is simply becoming aware. You will discover as you move through the LOA process that your awareness and clarity about your life will increase. Some people increase their clarity and awareness by leaps and bounds, and some people by increments. The good news is that everyone who follows through with this process develops heightened sensitivity and clarity about what's going on in their life. By completing the Self-Talk Exercise above (page 36), you have already completed the first two guidelines, which are:

1. You must understand what you are already saying to yourself, both positive and negative.

2. You must understand what was said to you in your childhood about yourself, both positive and negative.

If you did not complete the Self-Talk Exercise (and the preceding Inventory of Influence Exercise on page 34), please go back and complete them now. The LOA process is cumulative and builds on itself. Completing each exercise lends clarity and definition to the next exercise. Remember that there are only four written exercises, so I know that you can do it! You CAN complete each of the four written exercises.

"Be mindful of the words you use and the actions that you live and who you are and how it is you use your power. Keep clear at all times that you are what you say you are." -- Gary Zukav [4]

The third guideline is so important and so true that you will want to read it more than once. Read it three times and then let it soak in for an "ah-ha" moment.

3. Every declarative statement that you make about yourself or your life, whether positive or negative, is currently a working affirmation in your life, fueled by your belief.

Read the above statement two more times and really think about what this statement means.

To receive the full meaning of guideline number three, look back at your answers in the Self-Talk exercise. Look at your negative self-talk first. Are the items you listed as your negative self-talk manifested in your life currently, meaning right now? If you said to yourself, "I am broke," do you continuously find yourself "broke" ? Did you say, "Yes, they are manifesting" ? Ah-ha!

Now, look at the items you placed under your positive self-talk. Are these characteristics, qualities, or things currently manifested in your life? If you say "I am a good friend," are you "a good friend" ? Are you saying "Yes I am, and yes, these declarative statements are true for my life right now"? Now you're beginning to catch on! You're beginning to "catch my drift". The "golden nugget" of truth in this exercise is captured in guideline number three above. Read it again. This time it will really make sense to you. The fact is, you're already manifesting in your life. You've always been manifesting in your life, and *everything* currently in your life is something that you have manifested – either deliberately or unconsciously. The LOA process will teach you how to consciously manifest the things you desire in your life and will clarify for you the things you would like to move *out* of your life.

Guideline number four is important as you begin to write your affirmations for your life desires and goals. Pay very close attention to the technique of developing personal affirmations. *How* you write and say them is very important for them to manifest quickly.

4. Affirmations must always be written and stated in the positive affirmative.

This means you should write your affirmations using only positive, forward moving words.

Develop Irresistible Attraction

For example, you *would not* write your affirmation as:

"I will not weigh 190 lbs."

Instead, you *will* write it as follows:

"I weigh _____ lbs."

Fill in the blank with whatever weight is healthy and right for your age and body type.

Do not use the work "not" or any other negative word in your affirmation. This includes words like *debt, pain*, and *addiction*. You would not want to say: "I am debt-free," or "I am pain-free," or "I am free of addictions." Do you know the reason why? That's correct! Every time you state or write your affirmation, you and your subconscious mind will see the words: debt, pain, or addiction. Just like "Don't eat ice cream," your subconscious will pick up the negative words and/or meanings.

Instead, use "positive words" for what you desire freedom from.

Examples:

- ◆ **A "Global" Affirmation:**
  "I am experiencing overflowing prosperity and abundance in my life. I have manifested more than enough abundance and prosperity to meet my daily needs."

- ◆ **Specific Goal Affirmation:**
  "I have manifested _____ or greater dollars per month and I am open to other sources of abundance and prosperity as well by {date}_."

If you would like your prosperity to manifest in the energy exchange of money, you can enter a money amount. Write in a money amount that will more than cover your monthly expenses and pay off your bills (plus any additional money that you might desire to receive).

However, remember that abundance can come through other energy exchanges such as free gifts and bartering, or the exchange of talents and items. Therefore, if you place a money amount, I would recommend that you state that you are also open to your abundance and prosperity manifesting from other positive sources as well.

I can't tell you how many of my LOA workshop participants have received free gifts they weren't expecting when they began this process. Money is only an expression of energy exchange. Be open to all forms of positive energy exchange and many complimentary things will begin to manifest in your life.

5. Affirmations must be stated as if the desired goal *already* exists. It does *already* exist as "potential" in an energy state.

> *"It took me quite some time to realize that prayer is actually an affirmation of what already exists."* -- Iyanla Vanzant[5]

It is very important that you write and say your affirmations as if they already exist, because they do already exist somewhere in an energy state of one form or another. All you are doing is manifesting your desires into your life.

Remember, science teaches us that energy is neither created nor destroyed, but changes from one state to another. The ice cube is a perfect example. Ice cubes are made from water that has frozen. It was liquid before freezing into a solid. As it is melting, some of the water molecules evaporate into the air as a vapor or gas, and the rest melts back into a liquid. As the water molecules change states of existence, from a solid to a liquid and a gas, the same amount of water you began with still exists. The water was neither created nor destroyed, it just changed from one state to another depending on the temperature.

You may now be asking, how does this example apply to the affirmations for my life's goals and desires? It's time for another example. Let's say that you desire to acquire some very nice new dining room furniture for your home.

Develop Irresistible Attraction

You write your affirmation:

"I now have very nice dining room furniture made of solid cherry, that includes a matching table, six chairs, a buffet and a china cabinet."

Before energy was expended by carpenters to build this furniture, it existed in an energy state as lumber. Before energy was expended to cut and shape the lumber; it existed in the energy state of a cherry tree. Energy was also expended chopping and hauling the cherry tree. Before the energy existed as a cherry tree, it existed as a potential cherry tree in the form of a seed. Under the correct growing conditions, and with the correct nutrients and the right amount of energy expended by the sun, the energy state of a seed turned into a cherry tree. Guess where that tree ended up? That's right, in your dining room. It now exists in the energy state of beautiful furniture.

Therefore, you are perfectly correct in writing and stating the affirmations for your life's desires and goals as if they already exist, because they do already exist in one energy state or another. You are simply moving energy to manifest your goals into your life as the energy state you desire.

The Church calls this energy God's "grace" and states that the "faith of a mustard seed" is the vehicle for manifesting the energy into your life.

The key point of this guideline is to state the affirmation as if it has already manifested into your life and avoid the words "I want" and/or "I intend to." For example, if you say: "I **want** new dining room furniture," you will be left **wanting** new dining room furniture. The same applies to intent. If you say, "I **intend** to buy some dining room furniture," you will be left **intending** to buy some dining room furniture.

As stated before, you must say something like:

"I now have very nice dining room furniture made of solid cherry that includes a matching table, six chairs, a buffet and a china closet by __{date}__."

Leave the words "want" and "intend" out of your affirmations.

A word about "Intentions"

> *"Every action, thought and feeling is motivated by an intention, and that intention is a cause that exists as one with an effect."* - Gary Zukav [6]

Intentions are talked about quite a bit in literature, so I do want to clarify. Behind every behavior there is an intention. A researcher I once worked with said that "intention" is the second best predictor of future behavior, with "past behavior" being the first best predictor.

However, I do not recommend using the word "intention" or "intend to" in your affirmations because while it may be the second best predictor of future behavior, it means the "action" or "result" you desire is "in the future" and not "in the now." A very important part of writing your affirmations is writing them **as if they already exist** because they do in some energy state or another, so write them in the "now," not the "future."

It is also important to look at your intentions behind your behavior, because if you do, you can find out why you may be experiencing life difficulties. For example, if you volunteer every weekend at a soup kitchen for the homeless out of a feeling of "obligation" instead of feelings of "joy and compassion," you may develop resentment. The negative feelings of "obligation and resentment" will lower your "energy vibrations" allowing for other negative low vibrational things to happen in your life because "like attracts like."

As stated previously, scientists have found that thoughts have substance, and you can actually create your own reality (you *have* created your own reality). Guideline six is all about becoming clear on what you really desire.

6. You must be clear in what you desire by making it *detailed* and *measurable*.

Affirmations that are written vaguely tend to bounce energy around without ever manifesting. Some people say, "Well, I just put it in God's hands, and He's supposed to send me a husband or a wife." The problem with this kind of thinking is the fact that it's not God who needs clarity about who this person will be, it's **you**. If you never write down the attributes you would like your future husband or wife to possess, you might not recognize them as the right one even if God sent this person right up to your front door. That's why you need to detail your affirmations. It's not for God's benefit; it's for your benefit.

Listing these attributes is very powerful and clarifying. Part of the process of successful manifesting is being clear about what you desire to manifest. Even though you write the affirmation as if it already exists, you can still place a date on it.

For example:

♦ **Specific Goal Affirmation:**

   "I have a new 6,500 or more square foot home with five Master Bedrooms located with a lake view on a three acre or more wooded lot by August 2004."

The reason this works is that there is no linear time in eternity, therefore this home already exists. However, since our society organizes by linear time, we need to list a manifestation date. Again, God doesn't need a manifestation date; *we* do. Listing details and a manifestation date makes your affirmation measurable, so you will recognize it when it manifests.

7. You must become a "thought police," or you will easily revert to what is natural, and that could be making negative statements about yourself.

When you first begin your LOA journey, you may find yourself reverting back to negative self-talk. The good news is that you are becoming increasingly aware of your self-talk. The fact that you now recognize your negative self-talk is the first step. We all have people in our lives, family, friends, and/ or co-workers, whom we are accustomed to engaging in negative talk, including negative self-talk. You could avoid these people for a while, or you could have some fun with the process. Tell the people you associate with that you are trying something new with your self-talk. Ask them to catch you anytime you say something negative about yourself. After they catch you three times, you will pay for their lunch. Believe me, they will now be extremely diligent in monitoring your self-talk for you!

After buying a few too many lunches, you will become very motivated to monitor your self-talk, but don't be too hard on yourself when you don't get it right. If you've just thought one negative statement, say "cancel, cancel," and then say three positive statements. However, try and avoid accepting this as your long-term technique. Continue to work on talking, thinking and staying in the positive until it becomes your new way of being.

8. You must completely avoid hard times talk, like "We don't have any money," "I have more month than money," and/or "I'll never make money in this job." Also, be careful to avoid negative blanket statements like "oh, same old, same old."

Focus instead on your positive affirmations for your goals, desires and any boulders or doubts you may have.

9. Avoid reading anything, taking seriously, or exposing your mind to anything that is printed, filmed, or said that is contrary to prosperous thinking.

> *"Everything we do is infused with the energy with which we do it. If we're frantic, life will be frantic. If we're peaceful, life will be peaceful. And so our goal in any situation becomes inner peace. Our internal state determines our experience of our lives; our experiences do not determine our internal state."* -- Marianne Williamson [7]

It is important to assess your environment for posters, pictures, cartoons, and anything that is negative, even if it is funny. For example, my secretary at a previous job had a cartoon picture on her office wall of a completely stressed-out woman. Underneath the picture, the caption read, "I need a stress break." Interestingly enough, in that particular job, my secretary always felt stressed out and like she needed a "stress break." Not only her, but other secretaries from the same office would come to visit her, sit under the cartoon picture and talk about how stressed out they were. They even made mention on several occasions how they felt like that cartoon picture looked.

It is very important that you take care to design any environment where you spend a significant amount of time as serene, peaceful and positive as possible. Surround yourself with what you consider to be beautiful, as beauty calms people down. Make sure you surround yourself with pictures of your goals and affirmations. Also surround yourself with positive quotes that are uplifting to your spirit. Surround yourself with positive posters that say where you want to go and what you want to be and do.

This guideline also applies to the books, magazines, newspapers, and other print media you read; the Internet, the radio shows, tapes and CDs you listen to; the television shows you watch; and the movies you choose to see. Pay careful attention to your feelings and how you are affected by both the electronic and print media. If you find it upsetting to your spirit and draining your energy, you will want to find entertainment that is more uplifting and positive. This applies to educational materials as well. The material you feed your mind and soul should be chosen carefully, or you will end up with "mental and spiritual indigestion."

10. Never make a statement wishing evil upon another person. Never seek revenge, as it will "boomerang" back to you and "sit on your doorstep."

> *"Thoughts of vengeance, violence, and greed create emotions such as anger, hatred, jealousy and fear and lower the frequency of your Light, or consciousness. Creative or loving thoughts invoke high-frequency emotions such as appreciation, forgiveness and joy, and raise the frequency of your system. - Gary Zukav* [8]

Everyone has heard the cliché "What goes around, comes around." This is too true. Whatever energy you are directing out into the universe is what you are getting back, both good and bad.

Self-Talk and Affirmations

A LOA student told me he had given (with good feelings and good intentions) a family member some money. He knew at the time that the family member could not repay him. A few months later, he received some reward bonuses at work that more than equaled the amount of money he had given. This is an example of good energy boomeranging back.

My friend, Jeff, told me about a fun group exercise where all participants receive equal amounts of play money. They are told to give their money to other people as fast as they can. The winner is determined by who ends up with the most money when the bell rings. You would think it would be the person who hangs onto their play money. However, Jeff says that it's actually the person who is most successful at giving their money away the fastest. In the act of giving their money to other participants, other participants are more likely to give money back to them. Even if they are giving their money away so fast that some is falling on the floor, the most giving participant ends up with the most money at the end. The purpose of this exercise is to demonstrate not only what you give will come back to you, but also the concept that "You can't out give God or the Universe." When your intentions are pure, the good you give will return to you tenfold.

On the other hand, revenge and wishing evil boomerang back too, every time, in one form or another. This can create a vicious cycle and is all the stuff that fights, wars, and hurt feelings are made of. Just remember when you hurt another person or person(s), you are directly hurting yourself. The best illustration I have heard was a Chinese Proverb that stated, "I picked up a burning coal from a hot fire to throw at my enemy." The hot burning coal may or may not have hurt the person's enemy, but it most definitely burned their hand. Seeking revenge and wishing evil is the very same thing as "Picking up a burning piece of coal from a hot fire to throw at your enemy."

Seeking revenge and wishing evil also attract and manifest negativity. People who engage in this kind of behavior regularly will frequently report all kinds of "bad" things happening in their life, such as getting into car or other types of accidents, having their valuables stolen, missing valuable opportunities, and just generally finding themselves in the wrong place at the wrong time for bad things to happen to them.

It is worth many times over, going out of your way to wish others (even those you don't like) well, pray for their abundance and hold them in the light. When you do this, you bring light and abundance into your own life as well. What you do for others, you do for yourself.

11. Surround yourself with people that understand the importance of being positive.

These are people that make you feel energized when you are with them, not drained. When your energy level is high, positive affirmations work better and manifest more easily, and quickly.

Everyone knows someone who just drains their energy when they have been with them. I call this type of person an "energy vampire". When people are not open to receiving their energy from a positive spiritual source, they tend to try and steal other people's energy through various power and control tactics. They will try and get everyone to feel sorry for them, or they will try to intimidate others through their status, position, title, wealth, or knowledge. They may bully or threaten others physically or emotionally; or they will try to be the expert on every subject. They will talk nonstop and/or talk over others; or they will sulk and pout and won't reveal what they're angry about. They might even talk about others behind their back. These are just a few of the energy-zapping tactics some people use. I'm sure you can think of others. Even while I typed this information about energy vampires, I felt my energy drop just thinking about them.

To handle these energy vampires, you can choose one of three things: 1) avoid them like the plague, 2) be honest and tell them they are zapping your energy. Offer to teach them how to receive energy from a positive spiritual source through prayer and/or meditation so that they will no longer need to be an energy vampire, or 3) if they are someone such as your boss and/or you don't feel you can avoid them or be honest, you can pray for protection from their negativity and visualize yourself surrounded by the loving white light of God when they are around. You can also pray for them and hold them in the loving white light as well.

On the other hand, just think about the people that energize you and make you feel good. I call them "Earth Angels". When you think of them you smile, you want to be around them, talk with them, and be their friend. You look forward to the next time you will see them. You tell other people how wonderful they are, and you tell them how wonderful they are. You just want to be near them because they energize you. They may be your children, your significant other, your closest friends, other family members, a favorite teacher, a co-worker, your massage therapist, the secretary at your children's school, a friend from childhood, your pastor, your hairstylist, your florist, the parking deck attendant at your work, and any number of people in your life. Just thinking about the "Earth Angels" in my life energizes me. If you have one or more Earth Angels in your life, send them a note or email telling them so. You are a very fortunate person indeed.

12. Get to a "feeling place" with your affirmations.

> *"Our self-talk, for better or worse, affects our feelings. We tend to act our feelings – with words and/or behaviors. If we feel like winners, we act like winners… If we feel like losers we act like losers… Over time, we tend to become what we think about the most."* -- Dr. Louise Hart [9]

It's one thing to develop and correctly write affirmations; it's another thing to get to a "feeling place" with them. You *must* make your affirmations "real and alive" for you. You must *feel* them manifesting – touch, taste, smell, and hear their manifestation. Whatever way you can get to that feeling place, then do it. Place pictures on your refrigerator, photograph pictures of your desire, make a treasure map or collage of your desires/goals, visit stores, car dealerships, land for sale, whatever you can visit that relates to your desire.

Also, your desires/goals will manifest quicker if your energy is high. Spiritual energy is lighter and vibrates the fastest. How do you get spiritual energy? It's easy, you simply request it, demonstrate gratitude, and be open to it:

"Thank you God, for filling me with your love, light and spiritual energy."

It never runs dry and never runs out. You can always ask for a fill up. In addition, think of things that make you feel joyous and excited. Music, activities, people you love, your loving pets -- whatever is key for you, surround yourself by those things. When you are joyous, you are more open to receive the light vibrating spiritual energy, that will make your goals and dreams manifest easier and faster.

Sample Affirmations

Example of A Specific Behavioral, Measurable, Affirmation Used to Manifest Your Desired Goal:

"I have a new 3,600 or more square foot beach house with five Master Bedrooms, and all rooms having a beach front view by __{date}__ ."

"Thank you God that I am completely confident and firmly believe that ABC Company is manifesting well over $8,500 per month, or it's equivalent, in revenue by February 29, 2004 or sooner."

Your goal date must be believable to you. Otherwise, your unbelief will block your desired goal from manifesting. Therefore, you will need to write a goal date that sounds reasonable and believable when you read it.

Examples of Global Affirmations Used to Support Your Measurable Goal Affirmations but Not Used in Place of Them. *(See Appendix C for more Global Affirmations).*

Self-Talk and Affirmations

MONEY:

"I have more money than I need, and I feel good about that."

WEIGHT:

"I only eat a healthy variety of food that my body needs. I am slim, trim and attractive. My weight is now balanced and in harmony with my body."

It is very important after writing your affirmations to double check their wording making sure they do not contain any negative words like: will, want, intend, at least, debt, pain, addiction, the name of an illness and/or the name for any negative physical or emotional condition. Make sure all words are positive and forward-moving saying what you desire.

Rainer Maria Rilke [1]

"You must give birth to your images. They are the future waiting to be born ...fear not the strangeness you feel. The future must enter into you before it happens ...just wait for the birth...for the hour of new clarity."

PART II

Five Easy Steps to Getting What You Desire FAST!

Develop Irresistible Attraction

Wayne Dyer [2]

"When you can transcend your malaise and thoughts of impossible or incurable, and replace them with the energy of spirit where all things are possible, the material world responds and wholeness replaces visions of doom and separateness. Deliver this higher energy thinking to even the worst of circumstances and a spiritual solution is revealed."

CHAPTER 4
Manifesting What You Desire

Overview of The Five Steps

Listed here are the five easy steps to getting your desired goals met fast. In this chapter, I will first list the five steps. Next, I will explain what each step means, and lastly, I have provided a form on page 101 for you to complete the five steps.

Step 1. List your desires and goals (at least 3).

Write them in the form of a specific, measurable, behavioral, goal affirmation with a date for manifesting (See page 63).

Step 2. List any desires that you have already accomplished in your life.

Now compare these lists to both the positive and negative statements made about you or by you in the self-talk exercise on page 36. List any connections that you see between the statements and what you have accomplished in your life (See page 67).

Step 3. List any doubts/boulders/energy blocks to creating those Desires listed above.

This includes any perceived barriers to manifesting your desired goal. Turn them into a positive affirmation (these affirmations can be specific and measurable affirmations or global affirmations) (See page 69).

Step 4. Sensorialize your desires and get the energy moving

Part A -   Creating a Vacuum (See page 81).

Part B -   Invoking the Law of Forgiveness (See page 87).

Part C -   Making Your Desire Real to Your Five or More Senses (See page 95).

Step 5. Develop your personal LOA action plan for manifesting your desires into your life (See page 105).

The 5 steps are explained in Chapters 5 – 10 with each step having its own chapter. On page 101 is the blank worksheet that you will complete for the five steps. It is KEY Exercise Number 3. Please make sure you complete this worksheet. It will allow you to specify, clarify and detail your desires and goals by writing them down or typing them. Getting your desired goals down on paper is a very important part to manifesting quickly. Completing Exercise 3 is essential to activating the *Law of Attraction.* Then, move to Step 5, Exercise 4 on page 105.

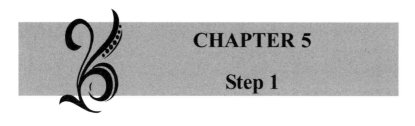

CHAPTER 5

Step 1

List Your Desires and Goals (at least three)

If you are not clear on what you desire, you can first make a list of what you do not desire. Once you have this list made, simply flip your "do not desires" around and that will give you your desires.

Then, write your desired goals in the form of an affirmation. Refer to the self-talk and affirmation guidelines in Chapter 3 if you need assistance.

Remember, to manifest quickly, you must be detailed and specific and write your affirmation for your desire as if it already exists in your life.

To do this, your affirmation can begin with any of these words:

I am ......

Thank you God/Spirit/Universe (your Higher Power) that ... ...

I am grateful that ......

I have ......

I affirm that ......

I have manifested ......

I am completely confident that ......

Specific measurable, behavioral goal affirmation regarding a promotion:

"Thank you, God, that I have received a promotion at my current job, including a raise of $1,000 or more per month by _{date}_."

Do you now understand how this goal is both specific and measurable? If this were your goal, you would be very clear when your promotion manifested because you have worded your goal with all the elements of a job promotion you desire. If you desire additional elements you might want to add some additional attributes such as working with charming, positive and supportive people. In fact, you may add as many specific attributes as you wish.

Don't worry that you have stated this goal as if you have already received it and then placed a due date on it because the clarity is for you, not God. Since there is no time in eternity, there is no conflict in placing a goal date as a part of your affirmation.

Specific measurable, behavioral goal affirmation regarding a romantic relationship:

"I am now dating a wonderful man/woman with these qualities: monogamous, between the ages of ____ and ____, having a sense of humor, reliable, responsible, dedicated, honest, healthy, fit, vivacious, nice-looking, compassionate, good dancer, romantic, positively spiritual, etc. by _{date}_."

As stated before, you must list the exact qualities you wish your significant other to possess; otherwise you may not recognize them when they appear. So many people say, "I just told God to send me somebody." Again, the clarification process is not for God, it's for you. God could send you the person that you were really looking for, and if you weren't clear on what that was, you might let them slip right by without even noticing them. Do not miss this important step of clarifying the qualities you are looking for in a significant other.

Step 1

So many people have come to my workshops looking for a significant other, that I have dedicated a whole section to relationships, including romantic relationships (see page 147). Romantic relationships are actually very simple to manifest. However, because most people have had some negative experiences in the past with these types of relationships, they need a little more assistance with this goal.

Develop Irresistible Attraction

Elbert Hubbard [1]

"All energy is divine."

CHAPTER 6

Step 2

List Any Desires That You Have Already Accomplished in Your Life

Then, compare these lists to both the positive and negative statements made about you, or by you, in the self-talk exercise on page 36. List any connections that you see between the statements and what you have accomplished in your life.

This is an important step because it will show you that you have already manifested many things you desire in your life. You will also find that for those things you have already manifested, you didn't have energy blocks/boulders/doubts around them (at the time of their manifestation). This may have made their achievement seem easy and effortless.

There are four main areas of life where people desire to manifest: **Relationships**, **Money**, **Career**, and **Health**. Most people manifest easily in two or three of these areas, and have difficulty with the remaining areas. If you look back over the self-talk exercise paying close attention to what you were told about yourself in childhood, you will most likely find that whichever of these four categories you are experiencing difficulties with, there was some kind of trouble in this area with the family that raised you. This "trouble" may have manifested between your parents, or between you and one or both parents, or even between you and one or more of your siblings.

On the flip side, in whatever areas you were supported, had positive feedback from your family, or had a good example by your family, you will find you manifest easily. For example, if you were told you were "smart and very good in school," but your parents were always fighting with each other over their perceived lack of money, you might grow up to advance easily in school, getting an advanced college degree, but have trouble holding on to money and have difficulty in romantic relationships.

Develop Irresistible Attraction

Sometimes, the messages you received in childhood can be confusing and insidious, such as the example I gave before about the participant that said his Mom had always told him "he could accomplish anything," but she also always told him to "be very careul, it's dangerous out in the world." She said that he could get hurt or even killed out there. This participant grew up trying to figure out why he had trouble concentrating on the projects that he really had a passion for. He would begin taking a class on something he was passionate about, but then wouldn't follow-up or complete the homework. In the LOA workshop, he discovered that this was due to his Mom's mixed messages about the world. She would tell him to "go for it," but then come back with, "but it is dangerous out there."

Again, notice how easily you advanced and manifested in the areas you were sure of and had no energy blocks, and how you struggle with the areas where you may have doubts/ boulders/energy blocks.

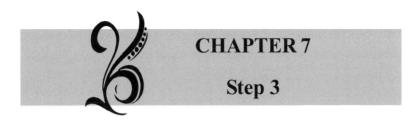

CHAPTER 7

Step 3

List Any Doubts/Boulders/Energy Blocks to Creating Your Desires and Goals

This includes any perceived barriers to manifesting your desired goal. Turn these doubts into a positive affirmation. Remove all doubt and replace it with "calm assurance" in order to demonstrate great faith.

> *"Like the mice, the two little people, Hem and Haw, also used their ability to think and learn from their past experiences. However, they relied on their complex brain to develop more sophisticated methods of finding Cheese. Sometimes they did well, but other times their powerful human beliefs and emotions took over and clouded the way they looked at things. It made life in the maze more complicated and challenging."* - Spencer Johnson, *"Who Moved My Cheese?"* [1]

The easiest way to complete this question is to think of any possible reasons that are, or could be, standing in the way of you manifesting your desired goal. These can be thought of as doubts/boulders/energy blocks or barriers. Whatever you call them, they have the same effect, which is blocking your desired goal from manifesting.

Identifying and removing doubts/boulders/energy blocks is the secret to making your desire/goals manifest quickly. If you had no energy blocks around your desires/goals, they would have already manifested. As mentioned previously, the main problem with most positive thinking and goal-setting courses is that they ask you to set your goals and be specific and list a date for attainment, but they never ask you how you "feel" about, and what your "self-talk" is about the goal you have set. For example, you might have listed that you would like a romantic relationship, but due to bad experiences with these types of relationships in your past, your underlying thought is "All men/women are jerks."

Develop Irresistible Attraction

When you have this thought, it makes you feel "bad" about romantic relationships. It also acts as a boulder, blocking the energy that is necessary for your desire to manifest.

I know this isn't the first time you heard that you must get rid of your doubts for your wish, prayer, or dream to come true. However, what we were not taught is the "how." We did not know quite how to identify doubts and then get rid of them. It was really just "hit and miss" as we went about trying to demonstrate the "great faith" we knew was needed for the answer to our prayers (and wishes) to manifest our dreams.

Now, you can learn the "how." First, you must be able to identify your doubts, boulders/energy blocks in your everyday self-talk.

How to Identify Your Energy Blocks/Boulders in Your Everyday Self-Talk

"Whether you believe you can or believe you can't, you're right." -- Henry Ford [2]

This negative self-talk actually blocks your desire from manifesting. If you're not sure what your blocks might be, think about the things you say as excuses, complaints and the reasons why "it just won't happen." These will give you a direct clue as to what your underlying beliefs are, and from there you can work to change them.

Any sentence that begins with these words, when referring to your desired goal can be identified as an energy block.

But...
If only...
I can't...

Step 3

It will take too much... (effort, time, money, skill...)
This is selfish/silly...
I'm too busy, too tired, too young, too old, too fat, too thin, too short, too tall...
It never happened when I tried before...
etc.

If I began a sentence with "I can't" when I was growing up, my mother always said "I can't, never could." I'm sure you've heard clichés like this yourself, and there is great truth in them. You can recognize your energy blocks by carefully observing your self-talk about your desire.

Obsessing and worrying about a desire is a huge boulder. Remember to replace obsessing and worrying with calm assurance that your desire has already manifested.

"Remove all doubt, have great faith." Again, these are admonitions we have heard many times before. However, what we were never told is what it felt like to have great faith – what it would look like in the 21st century to have great faith. Sometimes we just need a little more instruction to "get it." It's what I like to call "A fine tuning of the dial."

When you visit a restaurant and place your order, do you worry whether the waiter will deliver your meal? Do you hop up several times and run around looking for the waiter to make double sure he/she has placed your order? Do you rush into the kitchen to make sure the chef is preparing your food? No, you don't! Why? You "know" that if you have placed your order, your waiter will bring your food. It may not be exactly what you thought you were getting, and it may not be as fast as you would have liked, but you have "no doubt" that the waiter will bring you something of a food nature that at least resembles what you ordered. That is the feeling of "calm assurance" or "great faith" that I am talking about.

Also, do you have any doubt that you will have something to eat tomorrow? I have never had one single person in my workshop say they doubt they will have something to eat tomorrow, if they want it. Again, the feeling of "no doubt" about having something to eat tomorrow is the same kind of "no doubt" feeling you must develop about your desired goal.

> *"If the only prayer you say in your entire life is 'Thank you' that would suffice"* -- Meister Eckhart [3]

Interestingly enough, the tradition of saying "table grace" or a "table blessing" is the one area where we were taught to "Thank God" instead of "Ask God." Many people say "Thank You God for this food." They do not say, "God can you give me some food for today, tomorrow, forever." What I did not realize until I studied the *Law of Attraction* is that when we "Thank God" for our food, that is what is bringing us food *for tomorrow*. Thanking God yesterday, is what has brought us the food we are eating today. In other words, as long as we are "Thanking God" for what already exists, this demonstrates "calm assurance" or "no doubt" and we will be provided with more tomorrow and the next day and the next, as long as we "believe" we will eat tomorrow.

Other negative feelings in addition to obsessing and worrying can block our desires from manifesting.

> *"Crazy as it may sound, it's high time we woke up to the fact that we are electromagnetic beings tripping around with this mind boggling capacity to magnetize into our lives whatever in the world we desire by controlling the feelings that come from our thoughts. Our feelings go out from us in electromagnetic waves. Whatever frequency goes out will* [like a room full of tuning forks] *attract its identical frequency, thus causing things to happen – good or bad – by finding their matching vibrations. Happy high vibrations attract happy, high vibrational circumstances. Yucky, low vibrations attract yucky low vibrational circumstances."* -- Lynn Grabhorn [4]

Step 3

Please refer to Appendix B – Feeling Words Lists so that you may more easily identify what is a negative feeling versus a positive feeling. In Lynn Grabhorn's excellent book *Excuse Me Your Life is Waiting,* she details and clarifies how our "feelings" determine how we vibrate, and our vibratory level determines how we are manifesting. As I explained in the introduction, we are all made of energy, as is everything else. Not only does energy travel in waves, but scientists have now determined that energy also "vibrates". Lynn clearly explains that we are vibrating "magnets" of the universe. Positive feelings cause us to vibrate at a higher level, and vibrating high feels good because it is our natural spiritual state. Negative feelings make us vibrate low, which may make us feel bad, numb, or can even cause us to feel nothing because we may be so accustomed to vibrating low. As energetic magnets, we will attract people, circumstances or things according to where we are vibrating. So, if you have had what seems like a "run of bad luck," look where you're vibrating, as like attracts like.

> *"Trust allows you to follow your feelings through your defenses to their sources, and to bring to the light of consciousness those aspects of yourself that resist wholeness, that live in fear."* -- Gary Zukav [5]

The perfect example is my student "Jill," who began to feel like a victim when she lost millions of dollars in a lawsuit on a product she created that was stolen from her and marketed successfully. After that, she moved into a mobile home, had no job, and a possum died under her home, attracting black flies that filled the house. She also had her purse stolen, and had a hit and run on her car. She often told me that she would wake up and ask, "What will it be today, Lord? What kind of bad thing is going to happen to me today?" When she took my class, she learned the power of feelings associated with the word "victim". If you use the word "victim" to describe yourself, watch out! You will constantly attract low vibratory circumstances into your life.

We turned "Jill's" word and feelings around. She no longer used the word "victim" to describe herself; she turned it into the word "victor". In her mind and feelings, she went from manifesting as a "victim" to manifesting as a "victor". She wrote her positive affirmations around this new feeling of being a victor. She also invoked the

"*Law of Forgiveness*" (see the *Law of Forgiveness* on page 87), letting go of any negative energy feelings she had about the people that had stolen and marketed her product.

Before the fourth class was over, "Jill" went from having no job to having two new jobs! However, since these jobs were not her passion, she promptly got herself let go from both jobs on the same day. The good news is that she was then able to begin a successful business doing what she loves – helping other people. A year later she attended my LOA workshop again, set some new goals, and is now having her lawsuit reviewed. She has calm assurance that she is obtaining her highest good.

Believing You Need to "Work Hard" Is a Huge Boulder.

Remember – things do not need "hard work," they need belief.

> "*Old beliefs do not lead to new cheese.*" -- Spenser Johnson, *Who Moved My Cheese?*[6]

It is the "calm assurance and belief" that will bring all of the necessary events together to ensure that your desire manifests. If the exchange of money is a necessary ingredient in the desire manifesting, it is the belief and calm assurance that will allow all the money that you need to become available to you.

The first thing that I used to do when I wanted something new is figure out how much money it would take, and then figure out what kind of consulting job I could add to pay for it. (I already had six consulting jobs). As I began this LOA journey, I was pleasantly surprised to find that my students were manifesting many of their dreams without any need for the exchange of money. Free items would just come to them in one way or another. It seemed that when they were "in the flow" – meaning in proper alignment with the energy flow – people would just begin giving them things. In my last class, Joy, a piano teacher, demonstrated this energy flow quite well. She had found a partner, and they were beginning their own business teaching children and adults to play the piano. After she aligned herself properly with affirmations for the success of her business, and removed all her energy blocks, she received two free pianos, free piano books from a teacher who no longer needed them, and free space to teach from some doctors who had extra space in their office! She was absolutely thrilled that she was beginning a business and already had many students - all without placing a great amount of money up front. My students would tell me of constantly finding money on the ground, others would all of a sudden receive free coupons for events and activities. They received free clothes, free furniture, free vacations… the list goes on and on.

When I became serious about building the LOA business, the same thing began happening to me. In the past, my husband and I had, on more than one occasion, invested thousands of dollars trying to begin home businesses. My LOA business has never required money up front, and all the workshops I have provided have paid for any expenses and made money for both myself and the Church or organization where I presented.

I had always been told how difficult it is to find a publisher. Using the LOA system, not only was I introduced to a publisher, but they were also willing to actually wait on me to complete this book. I have not had to spend any time at all looking for a publisher, or an editor. When your desires come to you effortlessly, that is when you know you're "in the flow".

For those of us who always thought we had to "work hard" to realize our desires and dreams, getting "in the flow" can be fun and exciting. You don't have to call people anymore, they call you! You don't have to chase customers, they come to you! When you're "in the flow" you're operating by higher laws on a faster vibrational energy level, so things you desire manifest quicker and more easily than you could have ever imagined.

Removing the Blocks to Create What You Desire.

You can visualize your doubts as boulders, and then visualize a hammer breaking them up, and water washing them away. There are different tools you can use

Develop Irresistible Attraction

to help you rid yourself of doubts, energy blocks, or as we like to call them "boulders" in the stream of energy flow. It was actually one of my very first students that came up with the idea of calling energy blocks "boulders". In September 2001, during the third week of my first LOA class, we were trying to figure out why the students had manifested desires that they had been actively working on for several years, so quickly. My student Mal said, "Well, you know, doubts are like boulders in a stream, they block the energy flow like stream boulders block water. If we can remove these doubt boulders through faith, then our desires can manifest quickly."

When boulders are gone, our desires become in alignment "with the flow".

Some of the other strategies students have used to get rid of energy blocks are:

- ◆ Writing down your doubts and then throwing the piece of paper away.

- ◆ Writing your doubts on slips of paper and then inserting them in a balloon with helium and letting them float away.

- ◆ Visualize your doubts floating away in a balloon.

Getting rid of your "boulders" and having "calm assurance" that your desire has already manifested demonstrates great faith and is the key to meeting your goals quickly and easily.

Write a Letter to Your Boulder, Evicting It From Your Life.

When I took an acting class a few summers back, the teacher suggested a strategy for working with acting blocks. I thought the same advice would work for energy blocks or boulders to our goals, so I'm passing this good advice along to you.

Step 3

"I'm a big proponent of not judging our blocks. The blocks are there for a reason and may be helping us feel safe. I like the idea of inching our boundaries forward instead of full out changes. So, I suggest having some dialogues with your blocks. Write letters back and forth. Play the roles. Write short one act plays/dialogues. Get to know your blocks. Most of all, be kind to yourself and patient."-- Kenny Gannon[7]

For example, maybe you have an "energy block" about dating because you were so hurt by past relationships, or the men/women were "so boring or selfish," you are afraid of believing your affirmation about the "perfect man/woman coming into your life that you can marry and be happy with." You are actually blocking your energy by thinking that all men/women are selfish, boring or will hurt you - which you don't want! Remember, focusing on what you *do* want is the key to creating it.

You can actually *inch forward* towards your goal by changing your affirmation from a "life's partner" to a "safe friend" to go out with, have fun, have a nice companion to be with, etc. Then, when you've gone out with "safe friends" and you feel safe and good with that, you can inch forward a bit more and affirm that you are "Dating several nice men/women you are attracted to." When you feel safe with that, and have had some nice dates, and you feel ready, you can write the affirmation about your "life's partner". Don't push yourself; give yourself time (months or years if needed) to move through this inching process with relationships.

A letter to your Boulder/Block might read something like this ...

Dear Boulder:

I understand why you exist. I built you out of all the bad relationships I ever had. You're made of all the energy I ever expended crying in my pillow at night because "Another one bit the dust". I don't judge you, I was doing the best I could at the time with the information I had. I created you, and I can un-create you. You have served a purpose in my life; you have made me feel safe. However, now I am ready to move on. I'm ready to spread my wings again, ready to get out there and fly to the mountain tops.

78

Develop Irresistible Attraction

So, this is your eviction notice. No need to feel sad. You see, since you are composed of energy, I will break you up to become energy available again for more creation. It's called recycling! Only, this time your energy will be used in a new way. It will be used when I spread my wings; it will be used when I fly to the mountain tops.

Sincerely,

Your Creator

When you have completed your letter, visualize this process. Write the affirmation that you're ready for, and then put your plan into motion. Go out there and start talking to people about what you desire. People love to assist other people to make things happen in their life. They will know somebody who knows somebody, or they just found this great web site where your future date just detailed a five-page description of themselves. Talk your significant other into your life!

Turn Each of Your Doubts/Boulders Around into a Positive Affirmation and Write It Down.

Then, watch your language carefully. When you bring up a doubt/boulder either out loud to others or to yourself, immediately say your "affirmations." For example, "Jenny's" affirmation was:

"I now weigh 130 lbs, I am slim, trim and attractive by July 31st."

One of her main boulders was that she didn't like to cook and would grab fast foods that are high in fat and calories. However, she did know how to cook and found she only needed quick and easy recipes. The affirmation to her boulder was:

"I now cook quick and easy to prepare low fat, low calorie meals."

Step 3

On her "To Do" list she made a note to search on the Internet for easy to prepare low fat, low calorie meals.

Additional Affirmations

Some of your boulders may be covered in the main affirmation that directly manifests your desire. However, as in the previous example, write an individual affirmation for all the boulders you can.

For example, if your boulder is "I don't have time ......," your affirmation would be, "I now have all the time I need to ...." If your boulder is "I don't have the money.....," your affirmation would be "I have all the resources I need to......"

Notice I did not say "I have all the money I need to ......" The reason for this is that many times your desire will manifest from a source that doesn't require money. You need to leave your affirmations open to manifest from any positive source. **The "source" is the only thing you leave vague in your affirmations. Many times our desires will be met from a source we did not expect.**

If you cannot identify all your boulders, ask a friend or family member. Many times they can see in your life, or hear in your words some of the boulders you may not know you have. Just begin talking about your desire, and ask your friend or family member to tell you every time they hear you say a doubt or boulder type statement.

Once your boulders/doubts have been removed and you have the calm assurance your desire has manifested, BE PREPARED. Your desire will come true so fast, it will make your head spin. That is how you will know for sure that you do not need to remove any more boulders related to this specific desire.

Angela Monet[1]

"Those who danced were thought to be quite insane by those who could not hear the music."

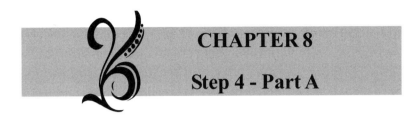

CHAPTER 8

Step 4 - Part A

Sensorialize and Get the Energy Moving through Creating a Vacuum or Space for Your Desire

Many of you have heard it said that "Nature abhors a vacuum". It's true for both physical laws and social or spiritual laws. We've all heard of the black holes in space and how any matter in their proximity gets pulled into the vacuum. One of the most beautiful sights I have ever visited is Crater Lake in Southern Oregon. The top blew off a volcano eons ago, created a vacuum, and now the top of the volcano is filled with crystal blue water. The crystal blue water filled the vacuum left by the volcano.

If you completely clear a piece of land with nothing left but bare soil, and come back in a year, will you still see clear land and bare soil? I dare say not. The land will be filled with weeds, grasses, small bushes, and saplings or small trees.

The good news is the "vacuum law" works just as well in the social and spiritual realm as it does in the physical. If you really have been trying to be prosperous, you've bought all the books and tapes, and have even been to some seminars and you're still not succeeding, it may be because you need to invoke the Vacuum Law of Prosperity.

In the *Dynamic Laws of Prosperity*, Catherine Ponder explains the Vacuum Law of Prosperity like this:

> *"If you want greater good, greater prosperity in your life, start form-*
> *ing a vacuum to receive it! In other words, get rid of what you don't*
> *want to make room for what you do want. If there are clothes in the*
> *closet, furniture in your home or office that no longer seem right for*
> *you; if there are people that you know, acquaintances or friends that*

no longer seem congenial — begin moving the tangibles and intan-gibles out of your life in the faith that you can have what you really want and desire. It may be difficult to know what you want until you get rid of what you don't want. Remember new substances do not flow easily into a cluttered situation." [2]

When the desires you have affirmed have not appeared, it is usually because you need to release and let go of something to make room for them. By letting go of the lesser, you automatically make room for your desires to come in.

When people are expecting company for the weekend, what do they do? Most people create a vacuum for their company to come into by cleaning a room for them and stocking the pantry with extra food.

When a couple is expecting a baby, they create a vacuum for the baby to come into by creating and decorating a nursery. We are very accustomed to creating a vacuum for certain events and activities in our lives, fully expecting those events and activities to manifest.

Before I began the LOA workshop, I remember desiring a new wardrobe, but not wanting to spend the money to buy one. I cleaned out my closet just to see how much room I could make. Not knowing I was creating a vacuum, lo and behold, my friend Cheri gave me a new wardrobe from her Mom, who had bought many fashionable clothes that she no longer wanted.

A lady that attended my workshop recently said she had manifested so many donated clothes she didn't know what to do. After she had more than she personally needed, she gave loads of clothes to charities. However, when she did that more and more clothes would appear! She literally had carts and boxes filled with clothes all over her living room. Finally, she had to an-nounce to everyone that her vacuum was full and she did not need any more clothes.

One of the men in my last workshop said he had heard about creating a vacuum several years' back and got rid of all the furniture in his living room. He said within a very short period of time his living room was again filled with furniture that had been given to him.

Here are some more examples of creating a vacuum for common desires that participants in the LOA workshops have listed:

Example – Attracting a Significant Other: If you want to have a significant other in your life, but you're still hanging on to an old relationship either actually, emotionally, or both, then your vacuum is full. There is no room for a brand new significant other to come into your life. You must create a vacuum by letting go of "Mr. or Ms. Wrong" to make room for "Mr. or Ms. Right."

I can remember dating guys just to have something to do while I was waiting around for Mr. Right. I never realized that I had filled my "vacuum" with Mr. Wrong so there was no room for Mr. Right to enter. If you are looking for Mr. or Ms. Right then definitely clear the way for them by having a "vacuum" ready and waiting.

Example – Working From Home: If your desire is to work out of your home, then you must create a home office with a home office telephone number and office furniture in a distinct area of your house. You must refer to your "home office" whenever you talk to your friends and acquaintances. Now, you have created a vacuum for your "work at home job" to come into.

My friend Cheri helped me teach the first LOA Class. Her goal for several years was to work from a home office so that she would have a more flexible schedule. She didn't enjoy reporting to an office every day for her job in sales. Our daughters are near the same age and have been playmates since they were toddlers. When my daughter and I were over visiting one time, I noticed Cheri had her computer in her daughter's room. I also noticed that she didn't have a home office anywhere in her house. I made the suggestion that she create a home office with a separate telephone number as a vacuum for her home business to come into. She said that would be easy as she already had an extra phone number. She began creating a home office that very evening, moving her computer into the space she had created. She then started telling others about her new home office. Within three weeks, she called me and said she was quitting her office job as she now had her own home business.

I realized that I had created the same thing when I had my second child. My daughter was in the first grade, and I felt it would be best if I worked from home. I had worked a full-time job from an office before my son was born. We already had a home office, so the vacuum was already in place. I got the word out that I was working from home and proceeded to manifest six different consulting jobs over the years in health and nursing education.

Example – Having More Peace and Balance: If you want to create a more peaceful and balanced life, you must create a vacuum in your home to experience what harmony and balance looks and feels like to you. This could be a meditation room, or an area of your bedroom or living room set up with fountains, relaxing pictures, relaxing music, and lovely plants. Or it could be a beautiful outdoor garden that you create. Let it be whatever comes to your mind when you think of peace and balance. Dedicate time each day to spend in this area you have created.

I love to have participants in my workshops describe their meditation or relaxation spaces to me. I can literally feel my muscles relax as they describe the beautiful areas they have created in their homes, set aside for the purpose of winding down, meditation, prayer, and reflection.

I encourage everyone to make a space like this that is a reflection of your own tastes and creativity. It can be just the corner of a room or it can be an entire room - whatever you have space for and desire.

Design it with your favorite colors and your favorite things. Place items that specifically speak to you about who you are, what you believe and what makes you feel relaxed. Then visit it often, especially when you feel the need for downtime to

Step 4 - Part A

center yourself, reflect, and just be. If you have a busy schedule, then actually make a vacuum by blocking out time specifically for visiting your meditation space.

Example – Relaxation Time: Some of my workshop participants desire more downtime as they want to enjoy a more rested, peaceful and balanced life. I suggest they create a vacuum by making an appointment with themselves on their schedule and actually reserve thirty minutes, several hours, or even a whole day once a week just to get their needs met and do the kinds of things that they like to do. They need to unwind to the point they actually "feel" relaxed. I can remember working so hard for so long in school, college, and then work, I didn't remember what it felt like to relax and unwind. Using my affirmation, I affirmed unwinding and feeling relaxed. I was so amazed at how good it felt. I was not consciously aware that I was always "on" for so many years, that I forgot where the "off" button was located and what it felt like to be "off". I know now, and try to get to that "off" place at least once a day. I also take one day a week as my "Sabbath day" where I spend time alone, praying, meditating, reading, and letting voice mail take my phone calls.

> *"Each person deserves a day away in which no problems are con-fronted, no solutions searched for. Each of us needs to withdraw from the cares which will not withdraw from us. A day away acts as a spring tonic. It can dispel rancor, transform indecisions and renew the spirit."* Maya Angelou [3]

One of the most enjoyable trips I have ever taken was to the beach with a group of five women for a silent retreat. It was coordinated by one of my sister-in-law's friends. She is a delightfully spiritual woman who said she was the love child of a priest and a nun. I thought, now this should make for interesting conversation when we do get to talk. The coordinator found an absolutely fabulous beach house where every bedroom had a beach front view with sliding glass doors and a patio or deck. I was in heaven.

We would not talk from the time we arose until 4:00 P.M. in the afternoon. We could read, meditate, enjoy the beach and ocean, listen to music, journal our thoughts, and make our breakfast and lunch; we just couldn't talk to one another

Develop Irresistible Attraction

until late afternoon. We took turns preparing supper, and when we did get a chance to talk we did a lot of it until bedtime. When I returned home after the weekend retreat, I felt like a "Humpty Dumpty who was put back together again by all the kings horses and all the kings men." I felt very peaceful, balanced and centered and most importantly, completely together. Since that silent retreat, I have not underestimated the importance of silence, meditation and reflection as a necessary part of my life.

Look at your list of desires. How can you create a vacuum that will assist your desires in manifesting? Add these ideas to your Action Plan To Do List (see page 106).

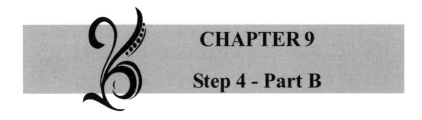

CHAPTER 9
Step 4 - Part B

Sensorialize and Get the Energy Moving by Invoking the *Law of Forgiveness*

> *"As it relates to forgiveness, you must give up what you do not want in order to make room for what you want. You must give up pain, anger, resentment and fear in order to experience goodness, joy, peace and love."* - Iyanla Vanzant [1]

Forgiveness is HUGE, HUGE, **HUGE!!!!** I cannot stress enough how important forgiveness is in your life. If you only hear and act on one principle I have taught, then make sure it's forgiveness.

I added the *Law of Forgiveness* to my LOA workshops when I realized that people were tying up and blocking much of the energy they needed to manifest their desired goals through their un-forgiveness. This was especially true for people that were either divorced or going through a divorce. I found they had a lot of anger and un-forgiveness towards their ex-spouse and any number of their ex's new significant others, whom they were sure were using money that rightfully belonged to them. Or conversely, they were now the second or third spouse who was giving all their money to their current spouse's ex whom (again) they were sure they were using it for their own pleasure and glory.

It was all about "Money and Ex's, and Ex's of Ex's, and Money," which I soon discovered from my LOA students do not make a good mixture. I found that many could not manifest well until they fully invoked the *Law of Forgiveness*. When they unleashed all the energy they had tied up in un-forgiveness, they all began manifesting like crazy.

Forgiveness Is Something You Do for Yourself.

First of all, most people have all the wrong ideas about forgiveness. They think that to forgive someone means what they did to you that hurt you was right. They think you have to contact the other person and get them involved. They think that forgiveness is something you do for other people; that it's a selfless act. While all this is very noble sounding, it's simply not true.

Forgiveness is actually a "selfish act." This doesn't mean it's a negative act. Far from being negative, it's actually one of the most loving and positive things you can do for yourself and others. This includes forgiving others as well as yourself.

I can remember the moment one of my LOA classes finally understood the concept that you forgive to bring "good" into your life, not for the other person. They said, "You really mean forgiveness is selfish? Oh good, then we'll do it."

"To forgive is to set the prisoner free, and then discover the prisoner was you." - Anonymous

Forgiveness Breaks A Bond of Negativity That Keeps Energy Tied up between You and Another Person or Persons.

Un-forgiveness acts as a kind of "energy dam". It keeps energy, which could be bringing good into your life, held up and immobile.

The negative energy between you and the person(s) of your un-forgiveness actually creates a bond between you that keeps you tied to them. The negative energy bond is stagnant and immobile and keeps you from your highest good.

Step 4 - Part B

Whom Should You Forgive? How Do You Know You Need to Forgive Someone? What If Someone Needs to Forgive You?

You should forgive everyone you can remember that you need to forgive from the sandbox right on up through today. This includes people who have already passed on, because it is possible you are still holding on to anger about injustices caused by someone no longer living.

You know you need to forgive someone if you feel (or think you might feel) anger, hurt, and/or resentment towards him or her. The first person that popped into your mind when you began this exercise is obviously the person you need to begin with. You then proceed in the order that people pop into your head. I can guarantee you that the person you're most angry, resentful and unforgiving of will pop into to your head – first and fast.

If you feel that you have hurt someone and you would like them to forgive you, you can still say the same affirmation of forgiveness on page 92. Simply substitute the words "I" or "Me" with either the word "You" or their name. You can still break the energy block and free energy by saying this affirmation.

You can also send them this book with the forgiveness section flagged and let them know you are asking for their forgiveness.

Upon Forgiveness, Energy Is Immediately Released to Bring Your Good.

When you invoke the *Law of Forgiveness,* the energy that has bonded you to them in a negative, stagnant way is immediately released and is now free to come into your life in a positive manner and bring your desires and highest good. There are always results from this important action and sometimes the results seem no less than miraculous.

Develop Irresistible Attraction

The Breaking of This Negative Bond and Releasing of This Energy Will Affect the Other Person(s) As Well.

> *"The great soul is the person who has taken on the task of change. If he or she is able to transcend fear, to act out of courage, the whole of its group will benefit and each one, in his or her own life, will be suddenly more courageous, though they may not see how or why."* - Gary Zukav [2]

While the other person(s) may not know what in the world hit them, they will experience the effects of the negative bond being broken and energy being released. The effects on them are usually positive as well. Their heart may be softened in ways people who describe them can't believe. You may even get a phone call, an email, a check, or even an apology right out of the blue. People who interact with those they have forgiven by invoking this law generally say that they are more positive, more pleasant and even nicer - some of them for the first time in years!

You Invoke the *Law of Forgiveness* by Saying and Making Real for You – Your Affirmations about Forgiveness.

An example affirmation is written on page 92 for you to use to invoke the *Law of Forgiveness*. To make it real for you, you must *feel sincere* about your forgiveness. In other words, you can't say something like, "I forgive you, you old so and so, I loose you, you mean thing, and let you go, you no good such and such person, etc, etc."

You Do Not Need to Contact the Other Person(s) to Let Them Know You Have Invoked the *Law of Forgiveness* Unless You Choose To.

It is not necessary to contact the other person or persons for you to invoke the *Law of Forgiveness* and for it to work. For example, for some people who were sexually abused as children, it may not even be appropriate to have

Step 4 - Part B

contact with the person they are forgiving. You can freely forgive as many people as you choose right in the privacy of your own home. Some people choose to contact the person(s) they are forgiving and that is fine too. However, this is not necessary for forgiveness to work. Usually, the person(s) for whom the forgiveness is being invoked is quite surprised to hear they are being so freely forgiven.

Forgiveness and Reconciliation of the Relationship Are Two Different Processes. You Do Not Have to Reconcile the Relationship in Order to Forgive.

"Forgiveness does not mean approval. It involves a willingness to see with new eyes – to understand and let go. They did what they did out of their own weakness. You did not deserve it. They could not teach you what they did not know. They could not give you what they did not have." - Dr. Louise Hart [3]

I am restating this because it is such an important point. Forgiveness is something you do for yourself. It doesn't mean the other person was correct in their actions that hurt you. If they were correct, they wouldn't have hurt you in the first place. You may or may not choose to reconcile the relationship; it's your choice. Forgiveness will work whether you choose to reconcile the relationship or not.

You Can Repeat the Affirmation of Forgiveness for the Same Person(s) As Many Times As You Need To.

Most people want to know whether one is time enough. Well, if you never see the person, it may be. However, if you are in frequent contact, my guess is that they are going to make you mad or hurt your feelings again at some point. So feel free to invoke the *Law of Forgiveness* as many times as you need to, even if you have to do it everyday.

Forgiveness Is Freeing. Imagine a Huge Boulder That Has Been Weighing You Down Is Removed from Your Shoulders or From around Your Neck.

When you have sincerely invoked the *Law of Forgiveness*, you are releasing so much powerful energy that it will feel like a huge weight or boulder is being removed from your shoulders or neck. Now you will feel lighter and freer than you have in a while. Enjoy the lightness, the vibrancy and the freedom forgiveness brings.

Self-Forgiveness.

It is just as important to forgive yourself as it is to forgive others. When you forgive yourself, energy is free to come into your life and bring your highest good and manifest your desired goals.

> *"The remarkable thing is that we really love our neighbor as ourselves; we do unto others as we do unto ourselves. We hate others when we hate ourselves. We are tolerant of others when we forgive ourselves. It is not love of self but hatred of self which is at the root of the troubles that afflict our world."* - Eric Holfer [4]

How to Invoke the *Law of Forgiveness.*

Holding the person you wish to forgive in your mind, your affirmation of forgiveness should be stated something like this:

> **"I forgive you completely and freely, I loose you and let you go. So, as far as I'm concerned, the incident that happened between us is finished forever. I wish the best for you, I wish for you your highest good, and I hold you in the light. I am free and you are free, and all again is well between us. Peace be with you."**
>
> *Adapted from Catherine Ponder [5]*

Step 4 - Part B

Take A Deep Breath, You Did It!!!!

Powerful Examples

Here are four examples of how the *Law of Forgiveness* has had an immediate impact on LOA students.

- Karen took the LOA workshop in January of 2002, and worked on several goals regarding business with success. After invoking the *Law of Forgiveness*, she received a check in the mail for $25,000 from a 10-year-old lawsuit that had been finally settled.
- "Janey's" goal was to receive $1,000. She had been in the class for two weeks when she invoked the *Law of Forgiveness*. The very next week, she received a check for $500 from her ex-husband who was unemployed and had never sent a child support payment in 13 years. Since that time, she received the other $500 in savings when she purchased a rare item she had desired for some time.
- After "Rhoda" invoked the *Law of Forgiveness* regarding her anger towards her husband, her business sales increased tremendously in one month. She also had a call that there were plans to sell her product to a large company that employs 45,000 people.
- "Torie" had a very dark childhood and held quite a few resentments towards her family because of it. After she invoked the *Law of Forgiveness* her relationship with them all completely changed. Friends called her that she hadn't heard from in years, and she no longer felt any anger towards her family. She said it was quite amazing! "Torie" felt peaceful for the first time in her life and could focus on the love she got from her family instead of the hate, anger and hurt. Her business then started to flourish. Money and clients began to flow in faster than she ever imagined!

Develop Irresistible Attraction

Yehuda Berg[1]

"A darkened auditorium must respond to the light of a single candle. But no matter how much more darkness one adds – say by enlarging the auditorium – no amount of darkness can snuff out the light."

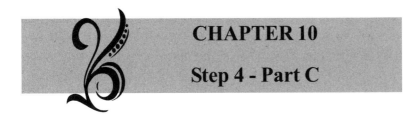

CHAPTER 10

Step 4 - Part C

Sensorialize Your Desires and Get the Energy Moving by Making Your Desires Real to Your Five or More Senses

This is the fun part. Here is where you get to muster all the boundless creativity you have to make your goals, dreams and desires come alive to your five or more senses. In this chapter, I will cover a few of the suggestions that participants have told me about to make their goals and desires real for them.

First, you will find it helpful to figure out the learning style that works best for you by reading the following descriptions. Visual, Auditory, and Kinesthetic are the predominant types of learning styles.

Visual Learner

If you are a Visual Learner, you like to "see" what you're learning. You may like pictures, graphs, maps, watching demonstrations, etc. You may be the one to notice if a public speaker has a button missing, needs to hem their pants or could use a "make-over". When you talk to others, you generally use words like "I see" or "show me it works," etc. It is easy for you to visualize your dreams and goals. You can easily see that "dream house" or "dream vacation" in your head. When I write the words "hot, gooey, chocolate sauce dripping over smooth, creamy, ice cream," an image of this is already in your head by the time you complete reading this sentence.

Develop Irresistible Attraction

Auditory Learner

You like to "hear" what you're learning. You learn best if someone "tells you the instructions," or by "listening to a speaker or teacher." You may enjoy listening to books on tape or CDs in your car as you are traveling. You may prefer someone explain driving directions to you, instead of looking at a map. You may enjoy listening to radio talk shows, or even listening to TV. You enjoy listening to a good story someone is sharing with you. You may enjoy talking on the phone. When you talk, you use words like "I hear you," or "Tell me about it." Learning through verbal or auditory communication is very important to you.

Kinesthetic Learner

You enjoy learning through active doing. You are "hands on" and prefer learning through actively participating. You learn best through your sense of touch and don't mind getting your hands dirty in pursuit of knowledge. You enjoy getting "a feel" for an activity. Your mind memorizes the way it "feels" to build, construct or repair an object, throw a pot, operate machinery, or dig in the dirt and plant trees, vegetables or flowers. You can tell if you're working correctly by the way it "feels" as it is coming together. You could still participate in productive work with your eyes closed and your ears plugged. When you talk you use words like "I just need to get a feel for it," or "Let me get a handle on it," or "It just needs the right touch."

Combinations

While most of us have a preferred method of learning, we may be using combinations of the three. You can actually rank these three in the order in which you use them. I am primarily a visual learner and can easily visualize in my head, but I also have a strong preference for auditory. I like to listen to interesting speakers and lecturers and don't mind taking copious notes. I would rather someone tell me driving instructions rather than look at a map. On repetitive activities, I rely on touch. When I practiced as a registered nurse, touch was very important in carrying out the numerous skills required to care for patients. I could actually feel if I had connected an intravenous medication (IV) correctly, set the IV pump correctlly,

Step 4 - Part C

or if I had moved a patient up in bed the correct amount.

Determine your preferences in order, and you will know what type of sensorial experiences will best work for you in manifesting your dreams and goals.

Once you determine your learning style, you will want to utilize that style to its fullest to manifest your goals. Also, try all the learning styles in addition to the one you prefer. You will create new nerve pathways in your brain by trying out styles other than your preference. Be creative… take chances, have fun!!

Ideas That Appeal to the Visual Learning Style

"Imagining myself enjoying new cheese even before I find it, leads me to it." From: *Who Moved My Cheese?*   -
Spencer Johnson, MD [2]

Use pictures from magazines representing your desires. Make them into a collage and/or place them on the refrigerator. Use Visualization, Role Playing, Writing Letters, etc.

Write a Christmas letter to your friends, dated December 19th (the current year) or the next year if it's December when you read this. Describe to them all your desires that have manifested in the past year. The students in my last workshop loved this exercise. Place the letter in a self-addressed, stamped envelope and mail it to yourself around December 19th. You will be surprised how much you have manifested just as you described in your letter.

Write a letter to your energy blocks evicting them (see page 76 for an example). Visualize your desire. What does it look like? How does it smell, feel, sound and taste? Visualize yourself bringing your desire home (if it's something that you can). Visualize yourself being happy with your desire. Write your affirmations on post-it notes and stick them all around your house.

Develop Irresistible Attraction

Some of my students like to stick them on their car visor. One of my students told me that looking up with your eyes at your affirmations will make them sink into your mind more deeply. Make sure your car is stopped before you look up at your affirmations!

Visualization

The process of Visualization will greatly increase your ability to manifest your desires. Essentially, this is the process of using your imagination to get in touch with the feelings that you will experience when your desire has manifested. In other words, it's something we all love to do anyway – daydreaming! This is similar to affirmations that are done before you achieve your desire because visualization is an internal affirmation that includes the feelings, sights, sounds, and everything that you will experience.

I'm sure most of us are aware of how athletes use visualization to improve their performance. We can probably remember seeing an ice skater or gymnast moving their arms and body in preparation for their routine. Many golfers say that they "see" the flight of the ball landing on the green before they hit their shot. The concept we are talking about is really no different, except that often you will not be visualizing a physical movement. You *are*, however, experiencing a desire that hasn't yet manifested on the physical plane.

There are many ways that this process can be done, including guided visualization and sitting in silence to name a few. In my workshops, I am able to work directly with a student to help them create a rich, detailed, and emotional image of how it will feel when their goal actually exists in their life. On the next page are a couple of samples that will help you get the flavor of what you want to do.

Remember that although this is technically a "visual" method, what makes it work is that you involve *all* of your senses internally. You *hear* yourself or others talking, you *see* yourself being successful, and most importantly you *feel* how it will feel.

Step 4 - Part C

Sample Visualizations

My friend, Jeff Brown, once had a student that wanted to meet and marry a man with whom she would happily share the rest of her life. Jeff had her picture herself sitting on an airplane (in first class of course), bound for her honeymoon in Hawaii, where she and her new husband were to spend two weeks on vacation. With her eyes closed, Jeff had her really experience how it would feel as they sat there holding hands, smiling, laughing, relaxing on the beaches, swimming with the dolphins, visiting historical sites and natural wonders, talking about their futures together, sharing the new-found love and joy that they shared.

Another student wanted more success in his sales job. Jeff had him visualize himself walking up to the podium at his company's annual convention to receive the award as the top salesperson for the year. He felt himself walking, saw and heard his coworkers and their families cheering for him, felt the love and support on his wife's smiling face. Reaching the podium, he shook the CEO's hand and received the award and thanks for all he had done for the company. He was then given a large bonus, plus a vacation for two to anywhere in the world. Now, how would that feel? These are just a few examples of visualization. As you can see, this technique can be a lot of fun.

Ideas That Appeal to the Auditory Learning Style

My teenaged daughter is an auditory learner, and I tell her that she came into the world talking. She said eight words at six months of age, and before that babbled constantly. The real strength for an auditory learner is their ability to "talk their desire into existence." Yes, it is completely possible to talk a desire into manifesting. You cannot know how many pairs of jeans my daughter has talked into existence. When you talk about a desire, not only do you create energy around it, but you also don't let other people forget it. Soon, your friends and relatives will be looking far and wide to assist you in manifesting your desire so that you may talk about something else for a change the next time you are in their company.

Talking a desire into existence also helps build your own belief system. Each time you talk about it, you remind yourself, increase your vibratory level, and announce it to the universe. Also, people tend to believe you if you are sincere and committed. Your friends and relatives will send all kinds of referrals in your direction to help you. As the energy begins to move, all types of synchronicities will begin to happen. It will almost seem uncanny at times, but you will be assured your desire is on its way into your life, and sure enough it arrives.

Auditory tapes are also popular with auditory learners. You can actually record your own voice saying your affirmations, and listen to the tape in your car. I have also been told that if you listen to your affirmation tape just before you fall asleep, the material sinks in deeper.

Morning people may wish to listen to their affirmation tape when they arise or while they're eating breakfast. Have fun with the tape. Record your affirmations with your favorite music to create an association in your mind. Now, every time you hear one of your favorite songs, you will think of your affirmation. Pavlov named this type of association Classical Conditioning.

Ideas That Appeal to the Kinesthetic Learning Style

The "touchy feely" group can have fun manifesting their desire. If your desire is material (like a new car) then by all means test-drive the car that appeals to you. Run your hands over the interior and notice how the steering wheel feels and how smoothly it drives. You should be able to touch most of the things you desire (or at the least a representation of your desire), except for a person, or something that stings or bites. I wouldn't recommend rubbing another person without getting their verbal permission in advance! All joking aside, I would definitely get "a feel" for your desire in whatever way is appropriate. I recommend that *everyone* do this – allow your inner self to enjoy how it will feel when your desire has manifested.

CHAPTER 11

Exercise 3 Worksheet

Key Exercise 3 – The Five Steps

Please complete this entire worksheet for Exercise 3. Do not skip this important task. Specifying, clarifying and detailing your desires and goals by writing them down are very important parts to manifesting quickly.

(After Completing Exercise Number 3, See Exercise Number 4 on page 105).

Step 1: List Your Desires and Goals (at least 3).

Write them in the form of a specific, measurable, behavioral, goal affirmation with a date for manifesting (see page 63).

1. _____

2. _____

3. _____

4. _____

Develop Irresistible Attraction

Step 2: List any Desires that you have already accomplished in your life (See page 67).

Now compare these lists to both the positive and negative statements made about you or by you in exercise #2 (see page 36). List any connections.

1. _____

2. _____

3. _____

Step 3: List any doubts/boulders/energy blocks to getting those Desires listed in Step 1 (See page 69).

This includes any perceived barriers to manifesting your desired goal, so that you can turn them into a positive affirmation. (These affirmations can be specific and measurable affirmations or global affirmations).

1. _____

2. _____

3. _____

Exercise 3 Worksheet

Step 4: Sensorialize your Desires and get the Energy Moving.

Part A: List ways you might create a vacuum to manifest your desired goal (See page 81).

1. _____

2. _____

3. _____

Part B: Make a list of the first three people you plan to forgive (See page 87).

1. _____

2. _____

3. _____

Part C: List 3 ideas for making your desired goal real to your five or more senses (See page 95).

1. _____

2. _____

3. _____

Step 5: Develop your LOA Personal Action Plan for manifesting your desires and into your life (See page 105).

Until One Is Committed

there is hesitancy,
the chance to draw back,
always ineffectiveness. Concerning
all acts of initiative (and creation), there
is one elementary truth, the ignorance of
which kills countless ideas and splendid plans:
that the moment one definitely commits oneself,
then Providence moves too. All sorts of things
occur to help one that would never otherwise have
occurred. A whole stream of events issues from the
decision, raising in one's favor all manner of
unforeseen incidents and meetings and material
assistance, which no man could have dreamt
would have come his way. I have learned a
deep respect for one of Goethe's couplets:
"Whatever you can do, or dream you can,
begin it / Boldness has genius, power,
and magic in it."

Quotation from The Scottish Himalayan Expedition,
By W.H. Murray, published by J.M. Dent & Sons, Ltd, 1951.

CHAPTER 12

Step 5

Key Exercise Number 4 Explained – Develop Your Personal LOA Action Plan for Manifesting Your Desires into Your Life

Completing this fourth and last form is absolutely key for manifesting your goals and desires quickly. Something real and concrete happens when a desire comes out of your brain and runs down your neck, arm and hand, through your pen, pencil, or computer keyboard (and printer) and onto paper. People who have manifested quickly and greatly will tell you that getting it down in writing not only clarified their goals for them, but also made the goals feel real and important. Also, you will have completed an activity that 90 percent of Americans never do: putting your goals and dreams in writing. **Use a separate form for each major goal**. Read the explanation for this activity, **and then complete the three forms that follow** (see page 110) with each of your three goal affirmations from Exercise 3, page 101.

Desired goal category

For the Desire Category, write the topic of your goal. Most goal topics fall into four categories: **Relationships**, **Money**, **Career**, or **Health**. If you want more peace, balance, or spirituality in your life, first ask yourself why those things are missing because you were born with them. Something must have happened between the time you were born and now for you to no longer have them, and thus to need them.

Peel back the onion and ask why you're not feeling peace, balance, or spirituality and you will find the reason in one of the four categories.

Develop Irresistible Attraction

Affirmation(s) for your desire

Write your affirmation from step 1 on page 101 here. Remember to write it as if it already exists because it does already exist in one energy state or another. You are merely manifesting it into your life. If you want to review how to create an effective affirmation, see Chapter 3.

Affirmations for any boulders/energy blocks

Bring over the affirmations you have written for any boulders from Step 3 page 102. An affirmation should be written for any boulders or energy blocks that are not covered by the affirmation for your desired goal. Do not bring over the words for your boulder(s), only the affirmation(s) for them. You do not want your brain to see the words for the actual boulder(s) everyday. For example, a participant of my last workshop had as a goal: *"I am now trim, toned, and fit, with my weight at _____ lbs, in balance with my body."* She had listed as her boulder that she doesn't have time to work out or exercise. For her affirmation for that boulder she wrote: *"I now have all the time I need to work out and tone my body."* List only your affirmations for your boulders, not the actual boulders as you don't want to look at your boulder in writing every day.

Action plan (to do list) for making your desires manifest

Your To Do List is an important part of the overall process. I always tell my students that you can't just lie on your bed and say, "I'm positive now, bring it on," and think all your desires will be met. Unless you are willing to have that relationship you're looking for with the pizza or UPS delivery person, you will need to get up, get going, and contribute to the process. You will contribute through your "To Do" list. This list will be the actions you will take to assist the energy that will begin to flow to make your desires and goals manifest.

Step 5

This action plan will, of course, include stating your affirmations however many times a day works for you. My students say them anywhere from three times to thirty or more times a day. Some say them every time they think about them or have a negative thought pop into their head.

Next, bring over the action items you listed for Step 4 on page 103. You will add to your To Do List, how you plan to create a vacuum, people you plan to forgive by repeating the forgiveness affirmation, and strategies for making your desired goal real to your five or more senses. Include as many of these strategies as you can.

Remember, this is an *Action* plan. If you're affirming getting a job, you will still want to send out resumes. If you are affirming a relationship, you will still want to attend functions and activities where single people of your "high vibrational level" will be found. If you're looking to boost your sales, you will still want to answer the extra phone calls and the extra email that you will now be receiving.

The energy will be moving to assist you in ways you couldn't have dreamed of, but you will still need to show up, be available, active and aware of where the energy is taking you. You will still need to have and work a "To Do" list.

Be aware of the synchronicities (smaller manifestations) that prove your desire is manifesting

> *"The universe is built to respond to our consciousness, but it will give back to us only the level of quality that we put in. Therefore, the process of discovering who we are and what we are here to do and of learning to follow the mysterious coincidences that can guide us is dependent, to a great extent, on our ability to stay positive and to find the silver lining in all events."* - James Redfield[1]

Carl Jung, a Swiss psychologist, defined synchronicity as "the perception of meaningful coincidence". Synchronicities are exciting because they are your first signs that the energy is moving to manifest your desired goal. Synchronicities are usually smaller manifestations that are proof positive your desire is materializing right before your eyes. Synchronicities can begin anytime, from almost immediately up to several weeks after you've begun the LOA process.

It is important that you increase your awareness to fully realize synchronicities as they are happening around you, or you can easily miss them. You may find that you "Can't see the forest for the trees." Since they may be subtle, you must look for them and be aware at all times. The more you practice, the more you will find numerous synchronicities.

My students will often describe the most major synchronicities, and then ask if they are important. Clara wanted to increase her private business and was called by the local newspaper to be featured as an excellent local businesswoman. She actually asked me if being featured in a newspaper that has a readership in the tens of thousands was a synchronicity. I'd say so, wouldn't you?

A synchronicity is any meaningful information that shows you the manifestation of your desire is on its way. It could be a book that jumps out at you in the bookstore, a friend giving you some related information, running into someone you haven't seen for a long time, a bumper sticker, a sign or license plate that has relevant information on it, etc. The sky is the limit!

Donna wanted to begin a Feng Shui business. This had been her passion for sometime. When she went to teach reading at a public school the next week, the librarian saw her in the hall and asked if she knew anything about Feng Shui as she was thinking of rearranging the library. Now, that's a synchronicity!

A workshop participant told me a story a while back as an example of a synchronicity and it really stuck in my memory. Several years ago, Eastern North Carolina (which is not far from where I live) was hit by Hurricane Floyd, and some people had to be rescued from the roofs of their homes due to extensive flooding. The participant said that his story was meant to teach a moral. The story was about a man stuck on the roof of his house after extensive flooding. He prayed to God to come and save him from the rising water. Soon, a man came by in a boat and offered him a ride. The man refused the ride, saying he was waiting for God to save him. After a while, a helicop-

Step 5

ter came by with a grab rope offering to carry the man to safety. He refused, telling the pilot that God was coming to save him. After a while longer, a man was floating by in a big inner tube and offered the man space to ride with him. For the third time, the man on the house refused saying that God was coming to rescue him. As the water continued to rise, the man on the roof cried out to God, "Where are you, why haven't you come to save me?" God answered by saying, "I came to save you three times and you didn't recognize me and refused my assistance."

I thought this was an excellent example of how we can get so caught up in looking for a specific outcome that we miss important synchronicities along the way. So, first we must be aware and sensitive to recognizing and responding to energy movement.

Date/time your desire manifested into your life and how you felt

It is important to record the date and time of your desired manifestation and how you felt in a journal. Then you can refer back to it as you write many more desired goals, and experience many more manifestations.

Action Plan Worksheets

On the following pages, you will find three Action Plan worksheets. Please complete one for each of your top three desired goals in priority, with the most important goal being listed as Goal Number 1.

Remember that taking action is absolutely necessary to attract your desires. Without having and using an Action Plan, you may have difficulty manifesting your desires. You will see that repeating your affirmations is one of the action steps.

I recommend you only work on one to three goals at a time. After manifesting your top three goals, you may write action plans for new goals.

Develop Irresistible Attraction

LOA ACTION PLAN FOR MANIFESTING YOUR DESIRES INTO YOUR LIFE

ACTION PLAN FOR DESIRED GOAL NUMBER 1

(Complete a Separate Form for Each of Your 3 Desired Goals)

DESIRED GOAL CATEGORY (money, career, health, relationship):

_____

_____

_____

AFFIRMATION(S) FOR DESIRED GOAL:

_____

_____

_____

AFFIRMATIONS FOR ANY BOULDERS/ENERGY BLOCKS:

_____

_____

_____

Step 5

ACTION PLAN (TO DO LIST) FOR MAKING YOUR DESIRE MANIFEST:

STATE AFFIRMATIONS _____ TIMES A DAY (3-30 or more).

1. _____

2. _____

3. _____

4. _____

5. _____

SYNCHRONICITIES (Smaller Manifestations) THAT PROVE YOUR DESIRE IS MANIFESTING:

1. _____

2. _____

3. _____

DATE/TIME YOUR DESIRE MANIFESTED INTO YOUR LIFE AND HOW YOU FELT:

_____

_____

Develop Irresistible Attraction

LOA ACTION PLAN (2)

ACTION PLAN FOR DESIRED GOAL NUMBER 2

DESIRED GOAL CATEGORY (money, career, health, relationship):

_____

_____

_____

AFFIRMATION(S) FOR DESIRED GOAL:

_____

_____

_____

AFFIRMATIONS FOR ANY BOULDERS/ENERGY BLOCKS:

_____

_____

_____

Step 5

ACTION PLAN (TO DO LIST) FOR MAKING YOUR DESIRE MANIFEST:

STATE AFFIRMATIONS ____ TIMES A DAY (3-30 or more).

1. _____

2. _____

3. _____

4. _____

5. _____

SYNCHRONICITIES (Smaller Manifestations) THAT PROVE YOUR DESIRE IS MANIFESTING:

1. _____

2. _____

3. _____

DATE/TIME YOUR DESIRE MANIFESTED INTO YOUR LIFE AND HOW YOU FELT:

_____

_____

Develop Irresistible Attraction

LOA ACTION PLAN (3)

ACTION PLAN FOR DESIRED GOAL NUMBER 3

DESIRED GOAL CATEGORY (money, career, health, relationship):

_____

_____

_____

AFFIRMATION(S) FOR DESIRED GOAL:

_____

_____

_____

AFFIRMATIONS FOR ANY BOULDERS/ENERGY BLOCKS:

_____

_____

_____

Step 5

ACTION PLAN (TO DO LIST) FOR MAKING YOUR DESIRE MANIFEST:

STATE AFFIRMATIONS _____ TIMES A DAY (3-30 or more).

1. _____

2. _____

3. _____

4. _____

5. _____

SYNCHRONICITIES (Smaller Manifestations) THAT PROVE YOUR DESIRE IS MANIFESTING:

1. _____

2. _____

3. _____

DATE/TIME YOUR DESIRE MANIFESTED INTO YOUR LIFE   AND HOW YOU FELT:

_____

_____

Colin C. Tipping [1]

"When a thought gathers sufficient energy to become a belief, it has an even greater effect in the world. It becomes an operating principle in our life, and we then create, effects – circumstances, situations, even physical events that hold true to the belief."

CHAPTER 13
Reworking Your LOA Plan

Reworking Your LOA Plan When Needed

What if you have written the affirmation for your goal correctly, so that it is specific, measurable, and behavioral with a goal date, and the date comes and goes with no manifestation? It could mean you need to uncover boulders you didn't know you have; you need to forgive someone (see chapter 9); you didn't really believe your goal date; or you need to create a vacuum (see chapter 8). After you have done all these things, you might need to reword your goal affirmation. Sometimes changing just one word or phrase will cause your desired goal to manifest quickly.

For example, my Mother and Father wanted to sell their house. They had already created a vacuum by moving into another house, and had invoked forgiveness and removed all boulders. My Mother wrote as her goal affirmation: **"Thank you God that our house on Pine Avenue has sold by February, 2003."**

In the several months that followed, plenty of people looked at the house, and some even tried to get a loan to buy it, but they all had bad credit. The result was that no one was able to obtain a loan to buy my parent's house, and thus it didn't sell.

I visited my parents at the end of July, and we realized that there was still another boulder. I told my Mama, "You're attracting people with bad credit, and you desire to attract people with *good* credit."

The new affirmation read: **"Thank you God that people with good credit have bought our house on Pine Avenue by August 4, 2003."**

118

Develop Irresistible Attraction

The phone rang the very next day with an offer to buy their house. Several people with "good credit" looked at the house and one of them purchased it. The purchase began on August 4, 2003.

People who are looking for romantic relationships are the LOA students that most often have to refine their goal. They will set a date for their affirmation, and then find they left a few important attributes out of their goal. So they reword their goal, set a date that meets that new goal, and wouldn't you know it - they left out a few more attributes, and so forth and so on. This goes on until they get their goal so finely tuned that they meet just the right person. Believe me, they become really clear on what they desire in a romantic relationship and/or life's partner by the end of this process. One of my first LOA students desired a romantic relationship that would lead to a life's partner. She went through this process of refining several times over the course of two years, and is now very happily married.

It is very important that you double check your affirmation(s) to make sure they do not contain any negative words like: will, want, intend, at least, debt, pain, addiction, the name of an illness and/or any negative physical or emotional condition.

If you have not met with success in manifesting your goal and you have removed boulders, forgiven everyone you know (even people you haven't met) and you have vacuumed your life inside out, take a look at what you **are attracting** and figure out what you **desire to be attracting.** Then you can change your goal and/or action steps to reflect what you desire to attract. You may need to refine the wording of your goal several times.

Keep trying, you'll get the wording just right, and BAM - here comes your goal!

PART III

Tools, Strategies, and Techniques for Assisting Your Desired Goals to Manifest Even Faster!

Develop Irresistible Attraction

Ron Rubin and Stuart Avery Gold[1]

"You were born with an innate capability to do, be and have all that your heart yearns for. There is something you're supposed to be doing and you mustn't waste another day ignoring it.

In order to be truly happy and completely fulfilled, you need to live a life designed around your own special talents and gifts."

CHAPTER 14
Keep the Energy/Synergies Flowing

You are now well on your way to accomplishing your grandest dreams and goals. In Parts I and II, you learned all the information you need to manifest whatever you desire quickly. Part III will give you all kinds of helpful hints, advice, ideas, and strategies. Many of these came from my students in the LOA workshops. They will help you manifest your goals and dreams even faster, and will help you to get rid of any energy blocks or boulders that you may have.

I will also cover the "Big Four" - **Money**, **Relationships**, **Career** and **Health**. These categories are the four main areas were my LOA students set their goals. Afterwards, I'll talk about some real examples and results from some of my LOA students. Please know that I have changed some of my student's names in the examples to protect their privacy.

When my student's have their energy vibrating high and they are manifesting like crazy, we refer to this very exciting phenomenon as *"Being In the Flow."* This means being in the energy flow. When someone is *"in the flow,"* his or her manifestations are happening one right after the other almost without effort. I think you'll find my students' experiences of *"being in the flow"* really exciting!

Keep Your Energy Elevated

For anyone that has ever had an authentic spiritual experience of any kind, you know that the energy you feel is wonderful and light. You feel peaceful, excited, yet calm, happy and even exuberant and blissful. You can receive spiritual energy anytime you feel you need it by simply affirming that you have it.

Develop Irresistible Attraction

"Thank you God/Spirit/Universe that I am now experiencing lots of good spiritual energy that I lovingly pass on to others. "

There is no limit to spiritual energy. God and the Universe never run dry. So, affirm anytime you need a tune up. You can also feel great amounts of blissful spiritual energy through practicing meditation.

As we discussed before, Lynn Grabhorn says (in her book *Excuse Me Your Life is Waiting*) that your thinking determines your feelings, your feelings determine your energy, and your energy determines how fast you're vibrating, which determines your reality.[2] This means that it is very important to be aware of what and how you're thinking, feeling, and vibrating. Also, you will attract into your life the people that are vibrating at your level. So, if you have ever wondered how in the world you could have attracted some of the significant others and friends you have, look at your vibratory level. You attract others according to how you think and feel about yourself. I will speak more about this in the section on Relationships (see page 147). This is all the more reason to get and keep your vibrations high.

Also, there are strategies available for increasing your vibration level by "getting your energy up." You know some of these already because you have already used them. A few examples include:

- Listening to your favorite music
- Talking to a favorite friend
- Taking a favorite walk in nature
- Watching a rainbow
- Seeing a double rainbow
- Reading a book to a child
- Listening to one of your favorite tapes as you drive
- Giving yourself a pep talk
- Receiving a pep talk from someone else
- Meditation/Prayer
- Giving and receiving hugs
- Yoga or your favorite exercise
- Seeing something beautiful
- Watching a waterfall

Keep The Energy/Synergies Flowing

- Reading a favorite positive book
- Listening to a favorite speaker
- Watching or participating in a favorite sport or activity
- Seeing your pets when they greet you after a long day
- Eating at a favorite restaurant that has just the right atmosphere and great food.
- Engaging in your passion

I'm sure you can think of many others.

When your energy is elevated, manifesting your desire is easier and occurs faster. This doesn't mean you can never have a down day. This is not "Howdy Doody" meets "Rebecca of Sunnybrook Farm" here. There are days when your spirit might feel low, and that's OK. Allow yourself to feel, grieve your losses and move on. One cute quote someone emailed to me said: "It's all right to sit on your pity pot every now and again. Just be sure to flush when you are done." I think that says it all. When you're done with feeling blue, don't forget to flush any residual negativity, and move on. Good times are awaiting!

Patrice Vecchione[1]

"What do I wish to believe in – my ability or inability? It was a novel realization when I began to see that I had a choice."

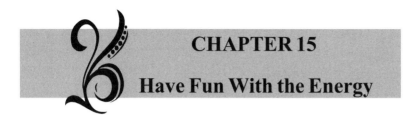

CHAPTER 15
Have Fun With the Energy

Playing With the Energy Keeps You "In The Flow" and Increases Your Belief

Fun and Amusing Exercises

"You have the ability and the power to increase your energy and access the highest/fastest energies for the purpose of eradicating any problems in your life." -- Wayne Dyer [2]

Engage in your favorite activities. Get your energy elevated, really up there, feeling good. Then, go to the mall or a shopping center. Walk into a store that is empty or almost empty. Start looking around and move around the store to spread your energy around. Then, stop and stare at something, anything. Within a few minutes you will notice that not only are people coming into the store, but one or two of them will stop beside you to either figure out what you're staring at (it could be a bargain you know) or to retrieve a product right beside the one you're staring at.

What's more, I am absolutely thrilled to tell you that "shopping" has now been scientifically proven to make you live longer. No more working out at the spa for hours, eating like a bird, and taking supplements whose names are weird acronyms. All you have to do is shop. Women have instinctively known this for years, and now they have the scientific proof to back it up. Guy McKhann and Marilyn Albert, two of the world's leading experts on brain research, began a 10-year study in 1985 of 3000 senior citizens to find out why some elderly live longer, more productive lives than others. They summarize their findings in their book, *Keep Your Brain Young (Wiley)*. The researchers say that shopping is a simple way to summarize what's good for the brain. It combines the three elements that allow the brain to function better: staying physically active, challenging the brain (shall I buy pink or blue?) and maintaining a positive self-image. [3]

Develop Irresistible Attraction

Let me clarify for the men that may be worried and confused at this point. When women go shopping, that doesn't necessarily equate to buying. Shopping and buying can be two separate processes. Now, you can all breathe a sigh of relief and read on.

All this shopping mall activity will increase your belief that the energy can work to manifest even your biggest desires. It also gives you a chance to play with the energy.

Finding a parking space right up front is another favorite of folks as they play with the energy. This works very well. Every Christmas the mall near my house is so full, people have to park across the street and walk a long way to get there. Last Christmas, I had to buy a heavy present, so I decided to "LOA" a parking space beside the door nearest the store I needed. I began saying my affirmation, **"Thank you, God I am parking in the front beside the door at this mall."** Then, I visualized the parking space and what it would feel and look like to park there. Lo and behold, with cars circling all around, a parking spot was waiting for me in front, right by the door I had requested. It was so wide, I thought at first it was a handicapped space. Then when I looked more closely, I saw it was not for the handicapped, but the space I had visualized. Cars were just driving right by it, not even noticing it. I have manifested numerous wonderful parking spaces in all kinds of locations, and you can too.

Stopping the rain is another favorite way people play with the energy. As many times as I have forgotten to bring my umbrella or lost my umbrella, I wish I had known years ago how simple it is to stop the rain for enough time to get into or out of the building to my car. I never worry now when I am caught without an umbrella, I simply either stop the rain, or slow it to a sprinkle.

I remember two times that I couldn't stop the rain. It worked to remind me that I shouldn't determine the source or timing. My goal is to stay dry in order to get to my car. I was affirming and visualizing stopping the rain one day, and nothing happened. Then, all of a sudden a very nice lady walked up beside me and offered me to get under her umbrella to walk to the parking deck. We had a very nice conversation, and I was able to give her needed directions to a building. Another time when I couldn't stop the rain right away, I ran into some friends in a store that I needed to see and had been thinking of recently. Just as soon as we completed

Have Fun with the Energy

our conversation, the rain slowed to a sprinkle, and I made it to my car. Remember, your goal is to stay dry, so if the rain doesn't stop for you, be open for whatever else is supposed to happen.

Watching movies about love (another boon for the ladies) has now been proven to activate a protective factor against colds and viruses. Dr. Bernie Siegel, in his longtime best-seller, *Love, Medicine and Miracles* [4], describes a 1982 research study by Harvard psychologists David McClelland and Carol Kirshnit, that found watching movies about love increased levels of immunoglobulin-A in the saliva of the human subjects for almost an hour. Immunoglobulin-A is the first line of defense against colds and other viral diseases. When shown a documentary of Mother Teresa's work, the researchers noted a sharp rise in immunoglobulin-A, especially in persons motivated by altruism. The researchers found this sharp rise independent of whether the subjects liked or disliked Mother Teresa. When shown a Nazi propaganda film and a short segment on gardening, no effect was shown in the subjects' saliva. The researchers also found the effect of the movies could be prolonged by having the subjects think about times in their lives when they had been nurtured by someone.

Dr. Siegel also points out, insurance companies have found that if a wife kisses her husband good-bye in the morning, he has fewer auto accidents and lives five years longer. Maybe, "kissing" could be used as a factor to lower your premiums. [5]

My guess is that kissing and watching movies about love (including the romantic variety) also increases our vibratory level and makes manifesting faster and easier. Researchers may discover the reason women live longer than men is not some magic effects of estrogen, but because of the magic effects of shopping, nurturing, and watching movies about love. To be fair, I certainly know men that do these things as well.

Laughing Hard and Having Fun Will Increase Your Vibrations

"There are sound scientific reasons why we call robust, unrestrained laughter 'hearty.' It produces complete, relaxed action of the diaphragm, exercising the lungs, increasing the blood's oxygen level, and gently toning the entire cardiovascular system. Norman Cousins [who cured himself of a terminal disease largely through laughter] *termed it 'internal jogging' and others have likened it to a deep massage."*- Bernie S. Siegel, M.D. [6]

Sometimes you just have to jump out of your ordinary and everyday existence and do something really crazy and fun (make sure it's legal). Do something with your friends that makes you laugh so hard you can barely stand it. I did exactly this to celebrate my mid-life crisis. Here is a section of my Christmas 2001 letter to family and friends describing the time I got together with Cheri, Christine, and some other girlfriends, and we all decided to become self-declared beauty queens in a small town parade:

Connie decided to celebrate her mid-life crisis this year with 7 other mid-life girlfriends by riding in the Pumpkin Parade in a small town in NC with a population of 1,200. We rode on a pontoon boat, turned into a float, all dressed as self-declared Beauty Queens. For the first time in its 50-year history, it rained cats and dogs during the Pumpkin Parade festivities and the Queens had a rather "drowned rat" look by the end of the parade. A leading town citizen and most eligible bachelor named Doug Dug escorted the Queens. Doug Dug owns a backhoe business (no kidding) whereby he takes his name. Get It? Doug – Dug!

After the parade, Connie and the other married queen returned to their castles, while the single queens visited a local bar named Ron's Motor Parts. They proceeded to be picked-up by another leading town citizen with a very big tractor whereby they took a ride around the town (on the very big tractor) - considered an exciting thing to do in this small town! You must be wondering, as were we, why the local town bar and hot spot for its two single men is named Ron's Motor Parts. We actually did inquire and the locals say "Because it used to be a motor parts before a bar, and nobody bothered to ever change the sign". That should give you a flavor for this fast-paced and progressive town, just down the road from Raleigh. After the parade, the Queen who hails from this small town was asked to run for Mayor.

This had to be the most hilarious adventure I've ever engaged in. I crowned myself the "Magnolia Blossom Queen of Prosperity." I was even thinking of prosperity as a Queen in the Pumpkin Parade! I wore the loveliest of green and gold sequined gowns, with a tiara of course, from my favorite vintage clothing store.

> *"There's just nothing better in life than to ride around on the back of a convertible* [or a pontoon boat] *with a crown on your head."* - Suzanne Sugarbaker of Designing Women [7]

I laughed so hard by the end of the day that my sides hurt. My husband and children stood on the parade route, in the rain, faithful as ever, watching their wife and mother living her life out loud. By the way, the book from whence this brilliant idea blossomed forth is called: *The Sweet Potato Queens Book of Love* by Jill Conner Browne, for women in, near or past mid-life. This book, while a bit risqué in spots, is packed with lots of laughs, ideas, and the most delicious recipes at the end.

While I was waiting for my life's calling to reveal itself, I decided to have even more fun and laughs. About this time, my girlfriend Sharyn and I, along with our associate minister Richard Maraj, decided it was high time we started an adult theatre group at our Church. We had always wanted to act, but didn't want to start in the chorus of our local community theatre because it was filled to the brim with people talented in the performing arts, many of whom actually had college degrees in theatre and voice. We didn't want to be in the chorus, we wanted to be the shining stars in our acting debut. So we formed the Unity Prime Time Players, and our first play was a Murder Mystery. My Mama asked, "You did a play about murder in Church?" Yes, we did, but the character didn't actually die, everybody just thought he did, so it didn't really count as a murder.

Develop Irresistible Attraction

We had such a good time being "stars" that we went on to produce and star in four or five more family friendly productions during the next several years. We had really caught the "acting bug," and just went "hog wild" with it. Soon we began an Arts and Entertainment Committee at our Church that celebrated the performing, visual, and literary artists in our congregation, and coordinated a variety show to showcase their talent. Sharyn even designed a page on the Church website to showcase all our talent and adventures. We even went on the road around Raleigh, taking our productions to another Church for their viewing pleasure.

What kicked off all this acting mania was the time my girlfriend Christine and I decided we just had to be extras in the movie *Patch Adams* (starring Robin Williams). After all, a feature film could not possibly be produced just 22 miles from our homes without our great acting talent sitting in the audience as extras smiling, laughing and even talking on cue. I actually had an action part where I stood up and then sat down at the beginning of one scene. We had such a blast! The cast and crew were extremely nice and accommodating, and we met so many wonderful and interesting people, including Ann from Raleigh, who has become another livelong girlfriend.

I was experiencing an excellent education on how to celebrate my mid-life crisis, laugh, have a good time and get my vibrations high. Then, lo and behold, sometime in the fall of 2002, God knocked on my door. My long-awaited calling had come. *The Law of Attraction* workshop, which I had been presenting for a year now, wasn't just to be another fun and interesting activity I engaged in at Church. It was to be "my calling," my service to the world. By this time, I had seen enough people who had demonstrated miraculous results with the LOA system that I knew it was what I was supposed to focus my talents and abilities on. In the months that have followed, I have never been so crystal clear about my life's purpose. For the first time, my complete life history, talents, abilities and even my issues make sense. All were preparing me for my calling.

Have Fun with the Energy

Work on Your LOA Plan of Action a Little Every Day

By now you have written a Plan of Action for three primary goals. This will assist you to stay "in the flow". Keep your plan of action in front of you and work on it a little everyday. Since your plan of action includes your affirmations, you should place them in a spot where you can clearly see them. This way you can recite them everyday, as many times as possible.

Make sure something gets checked off on your "To Do List" at least every other day. As you check off your To Do list, and say your affirmations, you will begin to see and feel the energy start to move. Increase your awareness to notice all the ways the energy is moving and write down any synchronicities that you experience.

Neale Donald Walsch [1]

Ultimately, self-realization is not achieved alone. Self-realization is achieved when we realize the self as seen in another. That is why all true masters do nothing but walk around, giving people back to themselves.

CHAPTER 16
Keep in the Flow With Your Mind Set

Develop an Attitude of Gratitude

"In our daily lives, we must see that it is not happiness that makes us grateful, but the gratefulness that makes us happy" - Albert Clarke [2]

Gratitude is BIG for staying in the flow. Being thankful for all that you have, will actually bring more your way. It is important to express thankfulness for all the good that you have attracted into your life. Sarah Ban Breathnach, in her bestselling book *Simple Abundance,* recommends a good way for feeling grateful to is keep a gratitude journal. You will want to select a book or notebook with blank pages to use for this purpose. It can be fancy with a fabric cover and sleek feeling pages or it can be plain and simple, whatever works best for you.

Keeping a gratitude journal can best be done by writing down at least three to five things a day that you are thankful for. This effort of writing three things everyday will change your life in a matter of a few weeks as it will become more and more difficult to "sweat the little stuff". You will discover blessings you didn't even know you had! I encourage you to set the following as one of your goals. For a year, write down three to five things a day that you are grateful for. It's fine to repeat things during the year. Everyday ask yourself "What are the three to five things I am most thankful for today?".

"As the months pass and you fill your journal with blessings, an inner shift in your reality will occur. Soon you will be delighted to discover how content and hopeful you are feeling. As you focus on the abundance rather than on the lack in your life, you will be designing a wonderful new blueprint for the future. This sense of fulfillment is gratitude at work, transforming your dreams into reality." - Sarah Ban Breathnach [3]

Develop Irresistible Attraction

Also, a very easy way to include gratitude into your daily lives is by expressing it through your affirmations. I originally taught people to begin their affirmations with the phrase: "Thank you God/Universe/Spirit/ (or their name for their higher power) …" because it was the easiest way to get them to write their affirmations as if their desire already exists – because it does already exist in one energy state or another.

When people write thank you notes, they write them for something that already exists or has taken place. When you write affirmations in this way, it is a unique way of expressing gratitude all the time. For traditional Christians (like my parents) I also found that the only real change they had to make in the daily prayer routine was "Thanking God" that the subject of their prayer had already come to pass instead of "Asking God". This mode of praying is completely supported in the Bible and does not go against the doctrine of any Church that I have been able to research. People of other religious traditions have told me that "Being Thankful" is completely in alignment with their teachings and beliefs as well.

My parents have begun to **thank** God instead of **asking** God in their daily prayers and have had tremendous success in that they have sold their home, obtained a new home, and my Dad had a physical healing. Through affirmative prayer, when many other strategies had failed, my Mom has been able to keep the deer from eating their backyard vegetable and flower garden. I will describe my parents' story in more detail under the section about health.

"When you go to bed at night, close your eyes and again be thankful for all the good in your life. It will bring more good in."
- Louise L. Hay [4]

Know That You Are Worthy

Worthiness is a theme that continues to come up in my workshops, especially among the women. Some people express they do not feel worthy of achieving their goals and desires. Like self-esteem, worthiness is an issue that will need us to "peel back the onion" and find out where this feeling originated.

Keep in the Flow with Your Mindset

As stated previously, I always tell people that they were born feeling worthy and with high self-esteem. If you don't believe me, spend a day with a two-year old. They have self-esteem, feel very worthy, and think they are the center of the universe. If you don't feel worthy as an adult, that means something happened between the time you were a two-year old and now. If you peel back the onion, you can discover what happened and turn it around.

Most often, I find that there are two main reasons people do not feel worthy.

- Someone they cared deeply about, like a parent or significant other, either told them they were not worthy or made them feel they weren't worthy.

- They were taught by their religion or philosophy of life they weren't worthy.

Some of us are fortunate to be born with a tough skin when it comes to what other people think of our worthiness. I can remember sitting in Church services as a child and hearing the minister say that we were "lower than a worm's belly" and were not even worthy of God's love. I am a visual person, so the first thing I would do is picture how low a worm belly would be to the Earth. I could see the worm traveling through the warm, brown, moist soil making it friendlier for growing plants. I can remember my brother catching earthworms and placing them in cartons after a big rain. These were fun memories for me as a child. I also knew that God loved me and the picture in my child's mind was of a loving, warm, gentle, grandfather figure. I could never replace that picture with a harsh, judging, angry God no matter what the minister said or how many times he said it. I just plain didn't believe him, not even as a child.

Another primary source of feeling unworthy is what has been said or implied to us over time by someone we cared deeply about. If your parent(s), significant other, or friends have told you negative things about yourself, you may feel unworthy. They may have even told you that you're not good enough. They may not have said it directly, just treated you as if you're not good enough. All this can add up over time, decreasing self-esteem and leading to feelings of unworthiness.

Well, I'm here today to tell you that you ARE worthy because you are made of "God energy" body and soul. What else could you be made of? You're worthy because the source of your being is worthy. To say that you're unworthy is to say God is unworthy, and this just isn't so. I read an epitaph one time that said, "I'm good inside and out cause God don't make junk." I think that just about says it all.

I love the following poem by Peter McWilliams. He was the favorite poet of the girls in my high school in the 1970s. His wise and poetic words gave expression to the myriad of emotions that formed our teenaged world. In one of his books, *Come with Me and Be My Life*, Peter McWilliams describes how his poems were recorded through guided writing. The divinity in this writing really shines through.

If you will notice, this poem begins with the words "I AM." These are two of the strongest words in our language. I encourage all my students to use the words "I AM" to begin as many of their affirmations as they can. However, please make sure that you place positive words behind the words "I AM" as these words announce to your mind, body, spirit and the world what you are. In the Old Testament of the Bible, the Hebrews recorded that God used the words "I AM" as self-identification. Peter McWilliams' entire poem can be used as a global affirmation to celebrate your worthiness. It makes me smile every time I say it!

I am worthy of my life and all the good that is in it.

I am worthy of my friends and their friendship.

I am worthy of spacious skies, amber waves of grain and purple mountain majesties above the fruited plain. (I am worthy, too, of the fruited plain).

I am worthy of a degree of happiness that could only be referred to as "sinful" in less-enlightened times.

I am worthy of creativity, sensitivity and appreciation.

I am worthy of peace of mind, peace on Earth, peace in the valley and a piece of the action.

I am worthy of God's presence in my life.

I am worthy of my love.

– Peter McWilliams [5]

Worry Not, Handle Your Concerns With LOA

How many times have you been told "don't worry"? How many times have you been told that it is a waste of time and energy for you to worry? Yet, when you try to not worry, your concern is still there. Telling someone to not worry is the "what" without giving them the "how". It is perfectly normal to have concerns during our Earthly journey. However, with LOA you now have a positive tool for addressing concerns that will eliminate the need to worry. When we worry, we create negative affirmations that actually work to keep our concerns fixed in time and space. For example if you say, "I run out of money before I run out of month," and you worry about that, the "worry energy" keeps your negative affirmation manifesting in your life. You will continue to run out of money before you run out of month.

With LOA, you state your desire, "To have plenty of money, and have money left over at the end of the month." Then you word your desire into an affirmation:

> ***"Thank you God/Spirit/Universe that my prosperity is abundant and I have more money than I need at the end of each month, {amount} or more, or money's equivalent, and I feel good about that by {date} ."***

Write down any blocks or negative self-talk you've been using, such as the negative affirmation in the first paragraph, to fully bring them into your awareness. This way you can rid yourself of them through your positive affirmation. Also, check your "worthiness thermometer". As previously discussed, many of us were taught by traditional religions (that view God as separate and outside of us) that we are "unworthy of God's love and grace," and "lower than a worm's belly". Many traditional religions also taught that "money is the root of all evil, life is supposed to be hard, and we are supposed to suffer."

The result of all this negative programming is that many of us grew up thinking we don't deserve great prosperity in our lives. If this is a "boulder/block" for you, then I suggest you identify and write affirmations about your worth. Repeat the "I Am Worthy" poem by Peter McWilliams (on page 136) until you feel worthy. Again, you are the energy of God/Spirit/Universe manifesting as a conscious spiritual and physical entity. It is impossible for you to be unworthy and separate from God. We can only *think* we are separate from God. To negatively affirm that you are unworthy is the same as affirming that God is unworthy. Examined in that light, the statement makes no sense.

"Remember, God is in you as the ocean is in the wave. There is no possible way in which the wave can be separated from the ocean, and there is no way in which you can be separated from God. Because you are the activity of God in manifestation, there is no place in all the world where you can get closer to God than where you are right now. You may become more aware of God, but you can never change this closeness which is the Presence of God in you. This is the great Truth that Jesus came to teach." - Eric Butterworth [6]

What a sense of empowerment it is to not only know we never have to worry about our concerns again, but to also know the exact steps we need to take to address them. All we have to do is change them into desires, affirm that the desire has already manifested, and then remove any doubts/boulder/blocks. Remember that the "Grace" of God is the "Energy Play Dough of the Universe." The Methodists call this "Provenient Grace," meaning God knows and has already answered our prayers. Through our thoughts/prayers/affirmations, and with God's full blessing, we can mold this energy into wavelength form, and then into actual physical reality. When you clearly state your thankful affirmation, your desire is manifested into energy form. Then when you remove boulders/energy blocks/ doubts, your desire is manifested onto the physical plane.

Mold, Create, Play, Enjoy – you are the otters of the Universe!

Develop Irresistible Attraction

Suze Orman [1]

"The road to financial freedom begins not in a bank or even in a financial planner's office like mine, but in your head. It begins with your thoughts."

CHAPTER 17

The Four Key Areas of Goal Setting

As previously stated, there are generally four areas where people set their goals. I call this the "Big Four" because everyone deals with these four areas in their life. Usually two or three of the big four areas go very well for them.

The areas that run smoothly are usually the ones where their parents gave them good feedback and where they have some natural skills, talents, and abilities. However, there are usually one or two areas where people are not manifesting as desired. For some reason, the person has developed energy blocks based on doubts and fears, and these blocks prevent them from manifesting smoothly.

These energy blocks may be formed in childhood, and are usually based on the teaching and fears of the person's parents or guardians. I have placed the big four in order of priority as listed by the participants in my workshops.

1. MONEY

2. RELATIONSHIPS

3. CAREER

4. HEALTH

Sometimes participants will list their desire as self-confidence, or they want more balance and peace in their life. While these are great goals, they are vague because they don't get to the reason the person is not experiencing self-esteem and self-confidence, or peace and balance already.

As discussed previously, we are all born with these. If a person is experiencing low self-esteem or a lack of self-confidence, this means that something has happened between the time they were young and now to decrease it. The same can be said about peace, harmony and balance. Have you ever watched a newborn baby sleep? There isn't a more peaceful picture on Earth than a sleeping baby. They look like angels.

If a person is out of harmony and balance, something had to happen between their birth and now for that to happen. I ask people with desires for peace, balance, harmony, and self-confidence to peel back the onion of their mind and emotions and write down why they feel they have developed low self-esteem or lack self-confidence. Why do they feel that they no longer have peace, harmony, and balance in their lives? Usually, they will shake their heads and affirm they already know what is at the bottom of their problem. Then I'll look into their eyes, hold their hands in mine, and say softly "It's a relationship that's at the bottom of this isn't it?" They will nod their heads in agreement and think I'm psychic for having figured that out. However, it's almost always a relationship that's at the bottom of these out of balance feelings, so I'm almost 99.9 percent guaranteed to be correct in my assessment. Even if someone says it's their job causing these feelings, peel back the onion another layer, and they will find relationships at work to still be at the bottom of the problem.

Then, I ask them to write their affirmations directly about the relationship that's causing them difficulty. Once they have a plan for addressing the relationship, their other affirmations fall neatly into place. Also, they will have quicker and more directed results.

Therefore, if it's not obvious which of the four categories your desired goal falls under, then peel back the onion and you will discover where you should be directing your affirmations. Also, your specific measurable and behavioral goals should never be written about a *feeling*, but about what it is causing that feeling.

CHAPTER 18

Goal Setting for Money

The majority of my students list money as their number one desired goal. The energy blocks people have around money are, to an extent, related to how money is viewed and interpreted by our society.

As a consequence of the Renaissance, the Protestant Reformation and the Enlightenment, Western society began to organize itself around trade, commerce, scientific achievement, and a more democratic government. All this makes money a key ingredient. This was not necessarily a bad thing and was certainly a step in the right direction - away from a society organized around a government run by either aristocracy or officials of a certain religion. If you ever visit a very diverse city such as New York City, you will notice that people of different ethnic backgrounds, religions, political beliefs, etc. can live peacefully side by side when their larger society is organized around trade and commerce. This shapes their interactions with one another into ones of economic interdependence and respect for each other's contributions. However, the moment the larger society and government becomes organized around one religion over another, or one social class over another, then all kind of trouble begins. No one can agree which religion the government should represent, or which social class should be "tops."

While organizing a society around trade and commerce can quell many political and religious squabbles amongst diverse groups of people, it can lead to a type of materialist view of the world. Also, the theocracies and monarchies (claiming the divine rights of the king) that many of the world's people lived under for years, taught them that money was bad and the root of all evil. I believe this was taught to the masses to keep them from revolting against the people in power, who also just happened to be the people with all the money. These negative teachings about money have followed people down through the ages and right into today.

Develop Irresistible Attraction

This history of how people have been taught to think and feel about money has created quite a dichotomy in their experience with it. As a result, many people have developed a kind of love/hate relationship with money. "I love money, but it is bad. I need money, but it may make me a bad person." When a person can't become clear in their head and heart about money, their wishes for money just bounce around the universe, and they do not consistently manifest what they truly desire.

We must become conscious and clear regarding our thoughts and feelings about money before we can consistency manifest it. Just like everything else, money is made of energy. The paper, ink, and coins themselves are made of the same energy as in any other material object. What money represents as a medium of trade is also a type of energy placed into motion. Money is no more and no less than a medium for the exchange of energy. Therefore, there is absolutely no reason to get all caught up with confused feelings about money.

In fact, just about anything could be used as a medium of exchange, it doesn't have to be money. My husband and I were in a baby-sitting co-op and used tickets as a medium of exchange. In co-ops (which means cooperative) time is frequently used as a medium of exchange. You donate so much of your time, and you receive credit that you can apply to purchasing baby-sitting, organic vegetables, fruit or whatever.

The most fascinating thing my students and I have discovered about LOA is that many times there is no requirement for the exchange of money at all. As previously discussed, my student Joy set as her goal that she has "A prosperous piano teaching business with her partner." She said her affirmations, and moved into the "flow of energy" and the equipment she needed for her business kept manifesting with no exchange of money required. The business where she had previously worked donated two pianos to her. Another piano teacher donated books and teaching materials to her. Some physicians donated office space. There were people that even donated time and assistance to help her make needed repairs to her office and get it ready.

Many times students find themselves manifesting with no money or very little money required to manifest their dream. Here is the story of my student

Goal Setting for Money

Christine who took the LOA workshop in 2002:

"I think I told you about the beginnings of my Autoharp project. Well, it's done now and I now have my diatonic Autoharp for a little over $200 because I converted it myself. (Buying a custom harp would be about $2,000 and getting someone to do it for me would be about $800). The whole time I got all the information and support I needed. I got connected to a lot of people in the Autoharp community. This really was the something extra for me. I learned so much. Other people I've met are very impressed I did it myself, but it felt easy because I had everything I needed all along.

I also have been teaching LOA to my kids and my son Aleks had a great demonstration. We had applied for a camp at the Science Museum and he didn't get in, and was instead put on the waiting list. We visualized him getting in and having a great time and kept that up for several months. They called a week before the camp started and said he was in. The whole thing was just perfect – we got free parking the first day and on and on. Thanks!" Christine

I had the wonderful experience of manifesting two family vacations this past summer with very little exchange of money required, and neither vacation involved sitting through a sales presentation about a time-share or retirement community. For the first vacation, one of the clients I consult with asked me to give a fifty-minute talk to a group of teen leaders and their parents about how alcohol affects the body systems. I was well acquainted with the subject, as I had revised a curriculum for this same organization that covered this subject matter well. In addition to my consulting fee, the organization paid for my entire family: a hotel room for two nights, all meals, and tickets for a day at a local theme park.

The second vacation was coordinated by an organization I volunteer with. Their purpose is to teach parents about alcohol and other drug prevention, so the parents can, in turn, teach their children about it. This organization paid for a room at an extended stay hotel that had a pool, tennis courts, and hot tub and was located only a mile from the beach for an entire week! Each room had a kitchen, and the hotel supplied a full breakfast (not just donuts, coffee and juice) and a light supper. My lunches were covered by the organization. My family joined me for the week. I was in a workshop all week during the day, but in the evening I joined my family for walks on the beach, visits to the ice cream shop and time together in the hot tub. During the day when I was in the workshop, my family had plenty of fun at the pool, the beach, and visiting local attractions. Other than a small amount of money my family spent on ice cream, a few toys, their lunches, and some local attractions, the entire vacation was covered in full including mileage … with no money exchange required.

The interesting thing is I had the thought that I would manifest a trip to the beach with my family this summer paid in full by one organization or other. Even though I didn't write it down, it still manifested. The only reason I say this is because sometimes, while actively manifesting the goals my students have detailed in writing, they will have a desire manifest they only had thought about. Don't misunderstand me here, writing down or typing your desired goals is an extremely important part of the LOA process, but when you get that energy moving, don't be surprised at all the good things that will begin happening in your life along with your manifesting your written goals.

I have so many students that have manifested so many things with little or no money exchanged that the list is too long to include. Therefore, when my students write their affirmations about money, I ask them to list a specific money amount and state, "this money amount or greater," and also to state "money or its equivalent".

As previously stated, the main point to remember is that money is just another form of energy in motion. In and of itself, it is neither good nor bad, but just a medium of exchange. This view has really assisted me in getting over my energy blocks about money. As a result, I have doubled my income in the last two years and will triple it or more this year.

CHAPTER 19

Goal Setting for Relationships

Creating the Romantic Relationship You Desire

"It is a risk to love
What if it doesn't work out?
Ah, but what if it does?"

- Peter McWilliams [1]

Keep Your Vibrations High

The second most popular desire in my workshops is relationships, primarily romantic relationships. Therefore, we will begin with romance. It is important to know that the people whom you have dated and married – you have attracted them into your life *based on how you feel about you*, not how you feel about them. You may think that is a strange statement, so allow me to give you an example. Have you ever had a friend that kept dating people that were abusive to them? I mean real jerks. You may have tried to tell them they deserved better treatment. Most of the time, they will notice that the people they date are abusive, but yet they cannot seem to figure out why.

We attract our significant others by how we are feeling about ourselves. People who date people that are abusive to them were often raised in homes where one or both their parents were abusive to the other, abusive toward their children, or both. While those who date or marry abusive people often recognize the abuse of their childhood, they don't realize they are allowing it to determine their current choices. When you don't feel very secure and sure of yourself, you will only feel comfortable around people who are vibrating in a similar manner. You may not enjoy the abuse, but it feels normal to you. When your friends try over and over again to introduce you to a nice person who will treat you well, you may find them boring or you don't feel that you're good enough to date them.

Before you can attract quality, nice people into your life, you must feel that you are a person who is nice and of quality yourself. Then, your whole vibration level will change. When you are walking down the street, or into a party, you will not even notice the abusive people, much less desire to connect with them. If you do find yourself in a conversation with one of these types of people, you will either consciously know that this is not a person you want to get involved with, or you will simply not have those feelings of connection with that person. It's all about feelings, and the vibrations that radiate those feelings to others.

Since the majority of my students writing a goal about a relationship are referring to creating the romantic variety, the first thing I ask them to do is to become very clear regarding the qualities of the person they desire to date. You must first become very clear about the character traits you desire this person to have.

Be Very Specific in Your Affirmation Goal Writing

If you affirm to God/Spirit/Universe your desire for a man, you will get a man. The same applies for those looking for a woman. God/Spirit/Universe will say "Here's a man." That's why you need to be a bit more particular. Some students in my classes say "But I have asked God for a man, and I am trusting Him to send me a man." As stated previously, my answer is that it's not God who needs to be clear on what kind of man you're looking for, it's you. If God sent you the man you are supposed to have, and you're not clear on what you desire in a man, you might not even recognize him when he walks right up to you and says "Hello". On the other hand, if you aren't clear about the characteristics you want in your partner, you may accept someone that is not right for you.

Your specific goal affirmation should read something like this:

"Thank you, God, that I am in a loving and fulfilling relationship with my ideal partner that possesses the following qualities... {fill in the blank} by {date}__ ."

Goal Setting for Relationships

Then list **ALL** the qualities you find attractive in a significant other. Example Qualities could be:

> Pleasant Personality
> Good sense of humor
> Shares values, including spiritual values, similar to mine
> Between the ages of _____ and _____
> Good looking
> Educated
> Single
> Has a positively balanced brain chemistry (meaning with no addictions, but don't use the word "addiction")

Continue until you have created a really detailed picture of your desired partner.

You may also want to create a separate paragraph/list that describes in detail *how the relationship between you* will be. In other words, the above list will cause you to attract a person who fits your qualifications, now you also want to declare that the interaction between you (the way the relationship feels and works) will be the way that you want. It will be supportive, trusting, loving, passionate, etc. Again, this is not for God, this is for you. How many people do you know who say they've found the perfect partner, but have many complaints about their relationship? Become clear on the relationship you deserve, too!

While you are attracting this person into your life, please make sure you state the word "single". One woman stated that she desired a husband, and she got one, but it was *somebody else's husband*! Also, be careful of the pictures that you place on your refrigerator. One woman placed a picture of a good-looking, tall man with salt and pepper hair on her refrigerator. Lo and behold, a tall, handsome man with salt and pepper hair came into her life. Unfortunately, he turned out to be an alcoholic. When she went back to rip the picture down from her refrigerator, she noticed the model was holding a mixed drink in his hand. Make sure the person in the picture you choose isn't holding addictive substances, another person, or anything else undesirable in their hands. The power of the image is strong.

Develop Irresistible Attraction

Create a Vacuum

I was explaining my LOA workshops to one of my students at my health education consulting job. Another student overheard only the part where I was talking about creating a vacuum. She said her last relationship had broken-up a year and a half ago. However, she and her ex-boyfriend would still go out occasionally as friends, and she still had his pictures up around her room, and the stuffed animals he had given her were still on her bed. She had noticed that even though she had felt ready to date someone else for some time, no one had asked her out. Her vacuum was full.

After she heard me talk about creating a vacuum, she went home and tore the pictures of her ex-boyfriend up, gathered up the stuffed animals he had given her and placed them in a plastic garbage bag which she carried out of her house and tossed in the dumpster. That very same day, only a few hours after she had created her vacuum, a guy that she had met several years ago called and asked her out. She really likes him and has been dating him for several months now. Again, to make room for Mr. or Ms. Right, you must evict Mr. or Ms. Wrong from your life completely.

Improving the Relationship You Have With Your Significant Other

> *"So one thing that partners do with and for each other is not seek to take from another, but seek to give to another, and to empower that other with whom you are partnered to express and experience who they really are."*- Neale Donald Walsch [2]

Quite often my students will desire to improve their current relationship. Most commonly, they are not feeling cherished, heard, and validated by their significant other. Some even feel that they have outgrown their relationship. Every student that has kept in touch with me and used the following affirmation has had results. The only thing I cannot promise is which direction the results will go. Your affirmation should read something like:

"I am now enjoying a deep, meaningful, trusting, and satisfying rela-

tionship with my significant other. I feel cherished and nurtured and validated by this relationship by {date} ."

If you repeat this affirmation often, within several weeks you will notice a change in your significant other. You will also notice a positive change in yourself and how you feel about yourself. Either they will begin to resonate with you as you vibrate higher and draw nearer to you, OR they will continue at their same vibratory level and may respond to your increased vibration level by drawing further away. If they draw further away, this will give you the information needed to make your next decision about this relationship. You can then decide where you want to go with it.

"Judy" attended several LOA workshops. She had experienced marriage troubles for years. Her husband had specific views regarding domestic roles based on gender, and expected her to fulfill a traditional role in their home. When Judy rebelled, her husband became angry and silent, often ignoring her for weeks. When she began saying the above affirmation, within several weeks her husband said he heard her concerns for the first time. Now mind you, she had stated her concerns to him over the years more times that she could count, but after she began saying her affirmations, he not only listened but actually heard what she had to say.

Most of my LOA students report improvements in their relationships after taking the LOA workshop and stating their affirmations. A few of my students, after gaining clarity, decided that it was time to move on from their current relationship. Some of them had written the qualities they desired in a significant other for the first time, and discovered that the person they were with, or had been with, met few, if any, of these qualities.

Improving Family Relationships

"There is a strong sense and connectedness in a family team. Members know that they are important, that they belong. Yet given the wings of independence, they are encouraged to find and create their own meaning and purpose in life, and to realize their own dreams." - Dr. Louise Hart [3]

This desire is so much fun because the most amazing things happen when an affirmation is written to improve family relationships.

During my second LOA workshop, a single mother's primary wish was for her two children (a boy and girl who are close in age) to quit their continuous fighting and bickering. She said they argued and picked on each other nonstop. Her affirmation read:

"My children enjoy a harmonious and loving relationship and get along well by __{date}__."

Then, she found of picture of her children smiling and hugging each other. She placed that picture at her desk at work and would look at it frequently and say her affirmation. She said she was absolutely thrilled when for the entire week since she began her affirmation, her children had not engaged in one single fight.

"Jane," a middle-aged woman, said that her elderly mother constantly complained and found fault with everything she did. She often dreaded visiting her mother due to her constant negativity. She said her mother had always had a negative outlook, but it had become worse with age. She wrote her affirmation for the specific weekend she was to visit her mother. It read:

"I am enjoying the visit with my mother this weekend, and she is joyful, happy and having a good time."

Upon visiting with her mother, Jane said that she was so surprised at her mother's turnaround, she actually questioned her to see if she was on a new medication to improve her mood. Her mother said she was not on any new medications, but was feeling better for some reason that she couldn't quite place her finger on. Jane said her mother did not complain once the entire weekend. This is the first time in Jane's entire life that she could remember her mother not complaining for this length of time.

Marianne said after the second week in the LOA workshop, she received more birthday cards from family and friends than she had ever received as an adult. She even heard from people that she had not heard from in years! One elderly mother was deeply saddened and depressed that she and her son had been estranged from some time. She wrote her affirmation:

"My relationship with my son is reconciled and once more loving and harmonious by {date} ."

The very next week, she received a letter in the mail from her son asking if he could visit her and make up.

"April" had a terrible relationship with her father. She said he was verbally abusive, controlling and constantly berating her. She felt obligated to him because he allowed her family to live rent-free in a house he owned. She began affirming her father treating her better, and invoked the *Law of Forgiveness*. She said several days after she began saying this affirmation, her father came over for a visit. Normally, he would have lit into her right away, but he didn't. While he didn't embrace her, for the first time she could remember, he didn't say anything abusive to her for the entire visit.

I decided to use LOA on my children. They were home all summer, with the exception of a few half-day camps. My daughter is fourteen and my son is seven. Most weeks were spent with quite a bit of bickering between them, and with them updating me frequently on the current state of their boredom. Due to the fact that I have a home office and work during the day, I could not provide continuous entertainment for them. We had just completed a two-week vacation, and I decided to use the LOA method to keep my children satisfied. They had only one week left before school began. I am very proud and excited to announce that it worked beautifully. My children did not bicker one time and my son did not say he was bored even once. My affirmation stated:

"Thank you God that my children are happy and content this week {date} at home finding many interesting projects and games to complete on their own."

Develop Irresistible Attraction

Watching the healing of families has to be one of the most satisfying aspects of teaching the LOA workshops. When a family heals, I believe humanity itself moves one step closer to healing and wholeness.

Improving Work Relationships

> *"A leader is best when people barely know that he exists, not so good when people obey and acclaim him, worse when they despise him. Fail to honor people, they fail to honor you. But of a good leader, who talks little, when his work is done, his aim fulfilled, they will all say, 'we did this ourselves'"*. -- Lao Tzu [4]

While romantic relationships are definitely the most popular desires for students in my LOA workshops, occasionally someone will be having enough trouble with a co-worker or two to list it as a top desire for improvement. The best thing about using the LOA method with co-workers is that you can actually get them to come to you to iron out your differences.

An LOA student was having trouble with two co-workers. He said his affirmation that "All is well between me and my co-workers (listing their names) and the work is flowing smoothly between us." Within a couple of days after beginning his affirmations, one co-worker actually came by his office and wanted to talk about how they could better work together, and the other one emailed him apologizing for having wronged him and also asked if they could make up their differences.

A student who took my LOA workshop at the beginning of the summer was having a difficult time with her secretary. She had tried to remedy the situation and was concerned that she was going to have to fire her. She wrote a similar affirmation to the one above and within two weeks, she said her secretary's attitude had significantly improved and they were working much better together.

Creating and Nurturing Friendships

> *"If I were to marry again tomorrow, I wouldn't give up one friend. I'd take them all with me as a sort of dowry and tell my new husband he was getting a rich wife"*. -- Merle Shain [5]

Goal Setting for Relationships

When I was a Brownie Scout, I used to love to sing the round: *"Make New Friends, But Keep the Old; One is Silver and the other one Gold."* I've also heard the saying "Friendships are golden". Friendships are frequently described like precious metals. I believe the emphasis is on the word "precious".

Lifelong friendships

When you have a good, kind, dependable friend, you can keep them for life. You are also a very fortunate person. I have several lifelong girlfriends including Christine, Cheri, Sharyn, and Ann, whom I've already mentioned. I met them all in the area where I currently live. My lifelong girlfriends: Lynn, Kathy and Dawn, I met in my twenties, and they live quite a distance from me. We communicate mostly by email and see each other a few times in each decade. My lifelong girlfriend, Mary, was a childhood friend of my husband, and a true Earth Angel. Another lifelong girlfriend, Sandy, I hear from at Christmas. My lifelong girlfriend from high school, Susan Gayle, I see at high school reunions and a few times in between. These lifelong girlfriends all tell me that "I know so much about them, they could never run for public office." However, the real truth is that they are all near and dear to my heart, and I couldn't imagine my life without their friendship.

I hope everyone has some friends they can count on for life. I intend to make lifelong friends of my two new girlfriends, Katharine and Donna.

Neighborhood friends and other friends and acquaintances

In addition to my lifelong girlfriends, Mike and I have "couple friends," male friends, church friends, work friends – students, faculty and staff, LOA friends, acquaintance friends, and just about any other category of friend there is. My massage therapist, Marge, is another one of those "Earth Angels" and friend. I also consider the other health practitioners I visit as friends.

We have neighborhood friends that come and go. The first thing I noticed when moving to our neighborhood is that no one was actually from our city. They were all transplants from New York – so much so, that I had to visit New York State to

Develop Irresistible Attraction

see if anyone still lived there! My husband also happens to be from New York, about fifty miles above New York City in Orange County. Therefore, he was happy as a peach and feeling right at home with our neighbors, all of whom have a last name ending in an "o" like ours. However, with so many transplants including my own household, there aren't many extended families around and making friends becomes imperative.

We developed many neighborhood activities when my daughter was small so that we could get to know our neighbors better. Then, the kids who were my daughter's age grew up and many families moved away.

In the mid 1990's to the early 2000's, just around the time that we didn't know any of our neighbors, we experienced two hurricanes in Raleigh, as well as a flood, a 22-inch snowstorm, and an ice storm that knocked out power for a week.

After a while, I began to notice that people pull together during a natural disaster. We had neighborhood cookouts using our defrosting meat, and went outside more when there was no power for air conditioning and lights. We spent more time talking and playing board games when there was no TV. The kids used the hilly road in front of our house to sled down the snow. During the ice storm, when we had no heat or electricity, our whole family crawled into our king-sized bed under a ton of blankets and comforters at 8:00 P.M. and talked until we fell asleep. We learned to heat coffee in our fireplace. Everything stopped, life moved slower and we all got a chance to catch our breath.

Don't get me wrong, I would not recommend affirming natural disasters as a way to meet your neighbors and make friends. However, what I did realize is how the architecture of our modern suburbs is built to keep people indoors and away from neighborhood interaction. I have heard that trend is changing with new architectural styles, such as neo-traditional and co-housing neighborhoods that encourage interaction. One time, I even looked (in vain) for assisted living for parents of young children. I thought how much easier it would be just to have that extra assistance. This would include help such as a cafeteria, recreation room, maid service, laundry service, pool and daycare on site that parents with young children so desperately need. Now that my kids are older, I feel less like I need assisted living, but I still desire and affirm to live in a neighborhood that has a small town feel and the architectural style encourages neighborly interactions. My affirmation is ...

> *"I live in a neighborhood with sidewalks on both sides, and front porches with rocking chairs, and a small quaint town section within walking distance, a coffee shop, a library, a neighborhood pool, and with many green areas where kids can play and neighbors can become friends, by August 2005."*

I didn't realize how endemic loneliness is in our culture until I started teaching LOA as many single people of all ages attend my workshops. When I heard singles begin to describe how lonely they are, I wondered what that was like. I had roommates after I left home and before I married. When I was twenty-two years old I did try to live by myself for three months, but within the first month, I had two marriage proposals and my roommate from my last apartment knocked on my door with suitcases in hand to move in with me. People would just not leave me alone, even for three months. Even though I turned down both marriage proposals, my roommate did move in. Now, with a husband, two children and a "hotdog" dog, I rarely experience a moment alone. However, I know there are people out there, many people in fact, who crave companionship. These are people who need some friends.

> *"Was I born to be alone?*
> *Is there someone in the darkness asking the same question?*
> *Are we each other's answer?"* -- Peter McWilliams [6]

Friendship With Your Higher Power

> *"God didn't stop speaking to us thousands of years ago, and He doesn't just talk to people such as the Pope and Mother Teresa. He talks to every single one of us everyday in thousands of ways. Some of us listen and some of us don't, but we are all born with the ability to hear him."* - Katharine Giovanni [7]

My very dear friend, Katharine Giovanni, has been a master at cultivating a friendship with God. In her book, *God Is That You?,* she describes her journey of

Develop Irresistible Attraction

loneliness growing up in a family that took the "fun" out of dysfunctional. She goes on to describe her search for God and how when she reached out, God was there and ready to talk.

> *"Stress can cause us all to do seemingly crazy things. Stress from money, illness or family problems can raise our blood pressures to an all-time high. God's friendship has helped me through many of life's crises, and it has made those hard times a little easier."* -- Katharine Giovanni [8]

In her book, she describes the simple process of how she learned to hear God's voice and how her friendship with God has continued to grow and blossom over the years. Now, as a very important part of her life's work, she teaches others a very simple process for having a two-way conversation with God.

My student Rayna described to the LOA class the very special relationship she has cultivated with nature. She describes how when she is experiencing wonders of the outdoors, she feels at peace and is most open to receiving spiritual communication through symbols found in nature.

Most participants say they can best listen for that "still small voice" when they become quiet and centered – either through meditation or prayer. I would encourage everyone to cultivate a friendship with his or her higher power. Then, you will know for certain that you have never been alone, and need never feel alone again.

> *"Do not suffer aloneness. There is no such thing."* -- Gary Zukav [9]

CHAPTER 20

Goal Setting for Career

"You should think of work as 'vocation,' which comes from the Latin word for 'calling' which comes from the word for 'voice.' ... work really should be – something that calls you, that gives voice to who you are and what you say to the world. If you find a vocation, embrace it. You will have found a way to contribute to the world with love." -- Kent Nerburn[1]

I began teaching LOA when the economy was in a downturn in September of 2001. Thousands of people in our area, known for high-tech companies, were being laid off. Finding a job was a big priority for many people. However, it was during this time that I found that jobs were one of the easiest things to manifest.

In addition to jobs, many people desired a new career. They desired to work in the area of their passion. They had worked plenty of jobs over the years and now wanted to work at what they truly love.

Manifesting Jobs

In attendance at my second LOA workshop was a single mom desperately looking for a job. She had been at home raising her children for seventeen years and was recently divorced. She had sent out numerous resumes during the previous month and a half without one single response. Her energy blocks/boulders were that she had been out of the work force too long and felt she had no skills She wondered who would hire someone like her. I helped her develop affirmations for getting a job and affirmations for her boulders.

Develop Irresistible Attraction

Her specific goal affirmation was:

"I am now employed in an enjoyable   {type}_ job with these responsi-
bilities: {list}   with a wonderful boss who possesses these qualities:
{list}   by   {date} ."

In addition, she created and said the following global affirmations for boulders:

"My life experience and work in the home has prepared me with all the
qualities I need to be successful in the workplace."

"I am a quick study and learning new skills comes easy to me."

This particular LOA workshop was four weeks long, with weekly two-hour classes. By the third class, she had received four phone calls asking her to interview. She also remembered a woman she once met at a Christmas party several years ago. She said at the time she felt she was meeting someone very important, but didn't know why. She had instant rapport with this woman and asked for her business card. She decided to call her and sure enough the woman from the Christmas party was looking to fill a job. The single mom went in for the job interview and got the job, with a boss that had all the qualities she was looking for, by the fourth LOA class.

Another LOA student was in a similar circumstance, except that she and her husband had been in business together and were now getting a divorce. She desired a job, weight loss, and a compatible man to date. She also desired that her husband treat her fairly during the divorce proceedings.

She said affirmations similar to those above, listing the qualities she wanted in her new boss. In addition, she also stated an affirmation about her husband treating

Goal Setting for Career

her fairly during the divorce proceedings. She also visualized him treating her fairly and said the forgiveness affirmation.

A short time later, she received a call for a job interview from a woman who had just recently bought a business and had found her resume stuffed in the bottom of a drawer under some other papers. She pulled out the resume and liked what she saw. When my student went to the interview, the woman was saying the exact things my student had written down in her goal affirmation for qualities she wanted in a boss. Furthermore, this woman was offered two more jobs, lost 15 pounds and found a compatiible man to date. On top of it all, her ex-husband treated her fairly during the divorce proceedings!

One gentleman who attended my second LOA workshop said he didn't want another job, just a promotion where he was working. He was so funny! When it was his turn to speak and share with the group what he had written in his exercises, he would simply say "ditto" to whatever the woman had said who went before him. In fact, he spent much of the workshop saying "ditto". When he came to the third LOA class, he told us that he got his job promotion. I think this was the only complete sentence I ever heard him say. He was happy as a lark. He was a man of few words who had gotten what he came for, and that was good enough for him. I never saw him again, but he sure had a big smile on his face when he left.

One of the most amazing accounts was of a woman who had been working for almost two years on getting a job in the pharmaceutical industry. Before she even attended the first LOA class, she said she felt an energy shift when she heard me advertise the class. The very next day, she was called and received a job making $150,000 a year. Truly Amazing!!!

Michael is a certified social worker working as a counselor, primarily with adolescents and their families. He desired a more flexible schedule, to make more money, and to be off in the summers. He had worked for the public school system and was now moving into private practice. Not only did he get everything he had written in his goal affirmation, but he was recently called by the school system he left, and was offered a handsome contract as a private consultant with flexible hours, plus he gets every summer off. Now he has a private practice with his former public school employer as a client.

Develop Irresistible Attraction

Michael's specific goal affirmation was simply:

"I am now employed in my own private practice as a certified social worker making {list} amount of money or more a month by {date}."

Manifesting the Career That You Love

After achieving his first set of goals, Michael attended his second LOA workshop and is now manifesting a greeting card business with a friend. Michael loves to write poetry and his friend is a photographer. They have joined as a team to create beautiful greeting cards. Michael is now manifesting one of his passions and making money at the same time.

Donna has a passion and talent for "clutter clearing". As mentioned previously, she is also interested in Feng Shui. For a number of years, she has been working at jobs, but none of them fit her passion. She has now begun a clutter clearing business and within just two weeks after the LOA workshop has several clients. She will help anyone who needs clutter cleared and a more organized house.

I have had many entrepreneurs attend my LOA workshops. Most of them have home-based businesses in Internet-based sales, network marketing, concierge services, real estate, or offering some sort of service, such as speaking, singing, photography, or playing/teaching a musical instrument. What they have in common is looking to increase their sales and business by using the LOA system. Their stories still amaze me at how quickly their businesses and sales increased during and after attending an LOA workshop.

Bill has a photography business and was a substitute teacher. By the third LOA class, he received a request for a $1,650 photography job and more business coming in. He had been called so many times to substitute teach he actually had to turn some down!

After just two weeks of LOA classes, Chris said his sales business had increased so much he didn't know what to do. When he found money lying on the ground, he saw this as a synchronicity or a sign of luck that his business was booming. He began finding more and more money on the ground and his sales business increased more and more.

Rosemary is a very successful distributor for a network marketing company that offers nutritional products and services tailored to meet the specific needs of each customer. Her sales increased 30 percent after only two weeks in the LOA workshop. They have continued to increase from there.

One sweet, dear lady named Evelyn has several home-based businesses. She said that after only one week in the LOA Class, she received eight new emails inquiring about the services she offers. I saw her at Church recently, and she said that the income from all her businesses had increased so much, she was too busy to even email me detailing her success.

Mary plays the harp professionally for weddings and events. After only two weeks in the LOA class, she had already begun receiving more requests for her business.

Finding Your Passion

All the people listed in the preceding section, Manifesting the Career that You Love, are making money in their passion. They tell me that when you work in your passion, most often it doesn't even feel like work. At times it seems effortless.

How can you tell if you're working in your passion? Well, if you hate your work, it's not your passion - that's one way. If your work feels very much like work and takes great effort, it's not your passion. If you have "TGIF" emblazoned across your forehead and are counting the days until Friday every week you go in, it's not your passion.

So what is your passion? Interestingly enough, your passion is generally aligned with your gift(s). It's the kind of thing you would even do for fun or a hobby. You might even be working in your passion right now as a volunteer or part-time. Your gifts are what you brought with you when you were born. You may have asked your folks for a certain musical instrument when you were very young. We noticed

Develop Irresistible Attraction

that our daughter could paint and draw far better than either one of us could when she was only four years old. She continues to demonstrate visual arts giftedness.

Your gift is the thing about which people have commented at different times in your life. They have asked you , "How do you do that?". When you're in your gift, your element, your passion, you seem to actually defy time. Many of us don't fully realize this because our gift comes so easily.

However, other people will comment on it and ask about it. Usually, your gift was noticed when you were very young, and your parents, your teachers, or your schoolmates complimented you on it. You may have even received an honor in school recognizing your talent such as best at sports, most likely to succeed, best dressed, most academically gifted, etc. Paul, another lifelong friend from high school, and I were recognized in our graduating annual as the "most talented" in our high school class. We both became health educators, public speakers and both act in amateur theatre.

If you think back, someone most likely recognized your gifts early on . I remember that I loved to write stories in elementary school. In fifth grade, I turned in a story and the teacher called me to her desk to ask me if I had copied it. I was absolutely shocked that the teacher would think my story was that good. I was also disappointed that instead of supporting me in my gift, she had suspecting me of copying. Look at the awards you have been given, the recognitions in your past. People will notice the talent of others early on.

I love to watch "Biography" on the A&E cable channel. After watching a number of biographies of famous people, it became obvious that their gifts were with them since they were born. It was generally recognized sometime in childhood. Their parents generally tried as best they could to support and accommodate their gifts by sending them to special schools and classes, and sometimes by even moving to areas of the country where their gifts could be most nurtured. Many times they were born into families with parents who had the same or similar gifts. If not their family, then a coach, mentor, teacher, or someone else close to them, recognized their gifts and became their supporter.

Goal Setting for Career

It takes a lot of courage to step out of your comfort zone and take a chance making a living with your gift. As a person who took that leap, I can tell you that you will not regret it. If you work in your gift, your passion, your element, the money will come. Also, you will help a great many people because you are in line with your soul's purpose. You will continually amaze people who will ask you, "How do you do that?". Just tell them, "It's my gift, and I'm here to share it with you."

Develop Irresistible Attraction

David R. Hawkins, M.D., PhD.[1]

"In every studied case of recovery from hopeless and untreatable disease, there has been this major shift in consciousness so that the attractor patterns that resulted in the pathologic process no longer dominated."

CHAPTER 21
Goal Setting for Health

I find it both interesting and surprising that health is always the last category cho-sen by LOA workshop participants. I have worked in the health field as a regis-tered nurse and health educator for several decades, so naturally I think that ev-eryone is always thinking of their health. My mother, an aunt, and a sister-in-law are all nurses. So, as you can imagine, there is a lot of health talk at our family gatherings.

My Daddy's Story of Healing

I am from a small town of 2000 residents. The town lies just at the end of the Chattahoochee River where it meets the Flynt River and then both become the Apalachicola River. My hometown lies where Georgia, Florida and Ala-bama meet. I actually tell folks that I am from North West Florida, where the Deep South ends. My parents still attend the same Southern Baptist Church I attended when I was growing up.

So why am I all of a sudden going into this family history at the end of the book under the health topic? Well, stick with me, I'm getting there.

When I first discovered how fast the LOA method worked for helping people meet their goals and desires, I was naturally excited to tell my parents. My daddy had had some health problems for some years, and my Mama had asked for prayers of healing for a blood clot in his right carotid artery. The carotid artery is one of two main arteries leading to the brain. If this blood clot broke off from the side of the artery, it could travel to his brain through the bloodstream and cause a stroke.

Now I knew Mama (being a traditional Christian) was not going to go along with words like "energy" and "getting in the flow" because every good Southern Bap-

Develop Irresistible Attraction

tist knows what Benn Johnson said so eloquently in his book, *American South: Celebrate Southerness Ya'll* is true:

"Jesus was a Jew on his mama's side, but his daddy was Southern Baptist." – Benn Johnson.[2]

So keeping this in mind, I developed an affirmative prayer making sure it was in line with Southern Baptist doctrine and language that she could repeat. The affirmative prayer read:

"Thank you God that James is healed and is continuing to heal."

I explained that she was simply *thanking* God instead of *asking* God, which "demonstrates the greatest faith". Especially since Jesus said, "*Your Father knows your needs before you ask him.*" (Matthew 6:8). Also, God said, "*Before they call, I will answer.*" (Isaiah 65:42*)*. For example, when someone has done you a very big favor like mowing your grass when you were on vacation, would you ask (after they have already cut it) if they would cut it? No, you *thank* them for mowing it. If God says He has already answered your prayers, wouldn't it make sense to *thank* God instead of asking Him, again?

> *"Have faith in God. I tell you the truth, if anyone says to this mountain, 'Go throw yourself into the sea,' and does not doubt in his heart, but believes that what he says will happen, it will be done for him. Therefore I tell you, whatever you ask for (claim) in prayer* **believe you have RECEIVED it,** *and it will be yours."* – (Mark 11: 22- 24) (Please note: The Greek and Hebrew words for "ask" also mean "claim")

Notice in the Bible verse above that Jesus says whatever you claim in prayer, believe you have **RECEIVED** it and it will be yours. Notice the **"ED"** on the word **RECEIVED**. Jesus doesn't say believe you "will receive" it. He says believe you "have **RECEIVED**" it. In other words, believe your prayer has *already* been answered. Powerful, powerful words that give us the key for our prayers manifesting quickly. In this one statement Jesus not only tells the "what" – Prayer, he explains the "how" to demonstrate the greatest faith to believe you have **RE-**

CEIVED it.

My daddy visited his doctor two months after Mama began the prayer affirmations. The doctor was quite amazed, and told my parents that not only had the blood clot totally disappeared in the right carotid artery, but the left carotid artery that had been 50% occluded with plaque, was now completely clear as well! The doctor was just about to ask for the tests to be repeated, when Mama interrupted him and said very politely in her southern drawl, "Now Doctor, my husband, James, has experienced a miracle healing from God, and you're just going to have to accept that."

> *"Thou shalt decree a thing and it shall be established unto thee, and light shall shine upon thy ways."* (Job 22:28, ASV)

Another LOA Student Heals

A student from a recent LOA class said he had very bad pain in one of his arms for two years and could hardly get around at times. He had sought help with no relief. After writing an affirmation that his arm was "healed and continuing to heal," he was led to a certain chiropractor. After one session with this chiropractor, he was pain-free for the first time in two years. I saw his partner recently, and she said he has also been led to a certain neurologist who had helped him as well.

I have noticed that for physical healings, after saying affirmations for him or herself or a loved one, healing either takes place on its own, or the person is led to someone in a healing profession who helps the healing occur. Definitely stay open to your source on this one. You should not list a specific route or person through which the healing will come. The healing may manifest in a manner or through a person you would not have guessed.

Also, remember that depending on your soul's purpose, healing may manifest in different ways. This could mean that healing for a person who has a terminal disease could come as a feeling of peace and contentment. If you say your healing affirmations for yourself or your loved one, removing all doubt, some type of healing will happen on some level.

Invoke the *Law of Forgiveness* to Heal

When I began graduate school in the mid-1980s, I started working part-time as a nurse on a hospital research floor for cancer patients. I noticed that these were the nicest patients I had ever cared for. I also noticed that when we did have an "ornery" patient admitted, they healed faster and sometimes would even be cured of the cancer. I asked other nurses about this, and they all noticed the same thing.

I had also heard that people who had a significant loss in their life and don't properly grieve, would develop cancer within two years of the loss. One evening, I asked my patients about this as I was caring for them, and was astonished to find that six out of seven of my patients had indeed experienced a significant loss (usually a death of a close family member) within two years of developing cancer. Every one of the six patients said they had not properly grieved their loss because they felt they must "stay strong" for other family members.

Now my observations in working with cancer patients are in no way even close to any kind of formal research, but I did come to two conclusions. The first is that you must properly grieve your losses – cry, talk about them, write about them, and get them out of your system. The second is to avoid stuffing any of your feelings and emotions inside yourself. The cancer patients I cared for were so nice and easy to care for because they often stuffed what they really felt inside, when they would have been much better off confronting people and situations and stating what was on their mind. After years of stuffing feelings, especially anger and re-sentment, cancer can develop. After a long nursing career, I have noticed that "mean and ornery" people rarely develop cancer, and on rare occasions when they do, many times the cancer won't kill them. They will end up dying of something else. You don't have to be "mean and ornery," the secret is to get your feelings out, instead of stuffing them down in your body, mind and spirit.

If you are a nice person who always places the feelings of others before your own, or you are a person with any kind of illness, especially cancer or an autoimmune disease (where the body turns on itself), ask yourself if you are feeling any anger or resentment in your life. If so, what is the situation that is causing these feelings and who is the person(s) behind that situation? Then, invoke the *Law of Forgive-ness* as many times as you need to *remove* and *release* this person, situation and these feelings from your body, mind and spirit. Also, talk to your body and tell it how much you love and care for it, and give your organs a pep talk. Visualize yourself as being well and whole, and your organs as happy and functioning freely. Don't hesitate to seek professional assistance with healing when needed. There are many healing practitioners that can assist you to *remove* and *release* negative disease producing patterns in your life.

The Mustard Seed Necklace

"You didn't have enough faith," Jesus told them. "I assure you, even if you had faith as small as a mustard seed you could say to this mountain, 'Move from here to there.' And it would move. Nothing would be impossible." (Matthew 17:20)

When I was little, my mama had the most wonderful necklace. It was a clear glass ball with a mustard seed inside hanging on a gold chain. It was my favorite of all her jewelry. When I asked her to tell me the story about the necklace, she would proceed to explain to me the story of the mustard seed. Even in my child's mind, I marveled that a person's faith need only be as big as a mustard seed to move mountains. Over the years in Church, I heard the story told and retold many times, and begin to wonder how, *How do you demonstrate the faith of a tiny mustard seed?*

After I began my LOA journey, it finally became crystal clear. A tiny mustard seed has all the potential already inside it to become a huge mustard tree. When it is placed in nourishing soil with proper water, it begins to demonstrate that potential. It doesn't worry whether it can become a huge mustard tree; it doesn't doubt its potential to become a huge mustard tree; it just simply allows itself to become one – to fulfill its purpose. It allows the process to happen without doubt, and without worry. When the sapling breaks through the earth and reaches for the sun, it allows the sun to do its work to feed and nourish it, along with the nutrient rich soil and water. There is no doubt in the mustard seed of its great potential. Jesus said that we can move mountains if we fully understand and demonstrate the calm assurance of a mustard seed.

Develop Irresistible Attraction

"Then Jesus said, 'Did I not tell you that if you BELIEVED , you would see the glory of God?' So, they took away the stone. Then Jesus looked up and said, 'Father I THANK you that you have heard me. I KNEW that you always hear me, but I said this for the benefit of the people standing here, that they may believe that you sent me.' When he had said this, Jesus called out in a loud voice, 'Lazarus come out!' The dead man came out, his hands and feet wrapped with strips of linen, and a cloth around his face. Jesus said to them, 'Take off the grave clothes and let him go.'" (John 11:40 – 44 RSV)

Notice when Jesus raised Lazarus from the dead that he "Thanked" God and "Believed" that his prayer had already been answered. Then he commanded Lazarus to rise from the dead. Notice that not once did Jesus ever "Ask" God or "Ask" Lazarus. He had great faith and calm assurance his prayer had already been answered. Somewhere down through the ages this all important technique Jesus used was lost to us. However, it has always been right there in front of us on the written page. We just need to "look with new eyes" to see it.

CHAPTER 22

Conclusion

The Transformation That Happens When Working With the *Law of Attraction*

Something dynamic happens when you catch a glimpse of the world Jesus was really talking about (the Kingdom Within). It can make you dangerous to the status quo. You become so transformed by the "Ah Ha, Now, I Get It!" that nothing else matters. For the first time, you've finally made sense of the whole thing, and you become as ecstatic as a child upon a new and exciting discovery. You can mold energy, you can "manifest stuff" you desire, "real stuff" into your life and fast, too. You must run and go tell your friends. Life suddenly becomes vibrantly awake and alive with possibilities. You wake up in the same bed, eat in the same kitchen, the same breakfast, go to the same work, with the same people, but nothing looks the same, nothing feels the same. Everything becomes vibrant with untapped potential, and you finally have the key (which is the knowledge) to unlock that potential. Like Dorothy in OZ, you suddenly realize you had the key all along, but if someone had told you then, you wouldn't have believed it.

That just about says it all. Thank you so much for entering this exciting journey with me. I look forward to hearing all about the wonderful things you have manifested into your life!

Blessings Abound!

Connie Domino

Appendices

Appendix A - Sample Success Stories

Here is a list of success stories experienced by my LOA students. Many of them have already been covered throughout the book. However, I thought that you might enjoy reading them in this consecutive format.

My mama's success continued

I have already told the story of my daddy's healing. I have also mentioned earlier in the book how my mama used the LOA affirmative prayer method to sell her house and rid deer from her gardens. Now my mama (like all mamas everywhere) knows what's best for her children, including me and my brother Steve, who is 20 months older than I am.

So when Mama manifested her desires, guess who she turned her new found praying abilities to next? You got it ... me!!!! Mama had been bugging me for months to take my children (Joanna and Matthew) to church. One of my churches has a nine o'clock and an eleven o'clock Sunday service. That summer, my children really wanted to sleep in, so my husband and I went to the nine o'clock service, and then out to a nice relaxing brunch with friends, and finally we would mosey on down to the Farmer's Market to pick up fresh fruit, vegetables, flowers and plants. We were just having a good ole' time dating on Sunday mornings. Well, Mama said she had heard of parents dropping their kids off at Sunday school and church, but she had never heard of parents going to church and leaving their kids at home.

She "put in" for us to take our children to church, which meant we would need to go to the later service and forget the date (of course, she didn't tell me she was doing this).

Well, lo and behold, my husband joined the church choir and would need to be at the later service to sing. It was the beginning of the school year and we decided to

Appendix A - Sample Success Stories

take our children to church since we had to go to the later service anyway. I just happened to be talking to Mama on the phone after all this transpired, inquiring about her manifesting. I told her she would be proud because Mike and I had taken the children to church. She was ecstatic, and exclaimed, "Oh good! Then it worked!", I asked, "What worked?". Mama said she and Daddy had been using the LOA Affirmative Prayer Technique to *"Thank Jesus/God that Mike and I were taking our children to church by the beginning of the school year."*

So the moral of this story is to watch carefully how well you teach the LOA technique to your Mama because I can just about "betcha" that when your mama gets her desires manifested, next she's going to "do you".

Now, I know what you're thinking. "Oh no, does that mean just anybody that wants can LOA me?" Fortunately, the answer is "No." Whatever happens as a result of anyone's thoughts or prayers about you, must be in line with your soul's purpose and journey in order to manifest. Taking my children to church happened to be in line with my (and their) soul's purpose and journey. Mama just brought it on.

Success stories from my earliest LOA Workshops - September 2001-2002

- A single Mom, after a long dry spell with very little dating, had three or four men as potential prospects and had been on dates with some of them. She was so excited that she could hardly sit still. She also had some wonderful things happening with a new business she was building. She made and shared a wonderful collage of pictures she found in magazines and pasted onto a poster board, making a visual representation of her affirmations for her desires.
- A student from my January 2002 class wanted a new building for a charter school in Southeast Raleigh that would serve underprivileged children. She is a volunteer there and was worried that since the economy was bad, there was not enough money for the new building. Plus her board of directors didn't support a new building. After attending the LOA course and applying the techniques, she emailed me to say that she got the building for her school and it opened August 18, 2002, just in time for the school year.
- Another student from the same class was recently divorced and had been

out of the job market for seventeen years. She had sent out numerous resumes without one response. She felt she was too old and had no skills. After only two weeks in the LOA Class, she had several calls for interviews and by the 4th week of the class, she had a job!

- A single mom, after several years of not dating, had a date with a man who met many of the things she had listed in her affirmation for a man she would like to date. However, he didn't meet the most important thing – to show an interest in her and her life, so she had to keep looking. However, she was very much encouraged by this date.

- A man's affirmation was to date and find love, and he did. He says he is absolutely in love. He introduced me to his new-found love at church.

- Another student was very excited about beginning a new business with her brother.

- A woman, after many months of not dating, had 3-4 phone calls after only her second week in the class. Since this time, she has had many dates and has dated several different men. She now feels that she has found someone with whom she can have a serious relationship.

- Another woman, after a dating dry spell, had three different men call her after only two weeks in the class. She is now dating one of those three. She has also sold several homes in her home refurbishing business. She is just about to sell a third home and is very excited.

- A man received a long-awaited promotion at his job after only two weeks in the class.

- Another man wanted to buy a refrigerator at 0% financing from Sears. Sears told him that they didn't have that option. However, he said his affirmations with calm assurance, and within several days Sears was offering 0% financing on their refrigerators. He also needed cat food one night when he was arriving home late and tired and didn't want to go to the store. He looked in his mailbox and lo and behold, there was one can of cat food sent as a promotion by a cat food company.

- An amazing story was of a student in the January 2002 class, who applied for a job months ago and said affirmations about the exact job she wanted. A lady called her months later after having found the woman's resume in a drawer after this business had been sold to another company. She liked the resume, called our class member and interviewed her. Our graduate said that the actual words coming from this lady's mouth were the same words she had written on her affirmation sheet.

Appendix A - Sample Success Stories

- A woman was so excited because she had been able to overcome some of the fears she had about prosperity and felt she would advance by leaps and bounds.
- A father was worried about the relationship between his 19-year-old daughter and a boy who was engaging in high-risk behaviors. The dad couldn't talk to his daughter or her friend, so he began saying affirmations that the best for all would manifest, and he developed calm assurance by removing energy blocks. Within two weeks the young man came over to his house and broke up with the daughter. She began dating a very nice young man.
- A student in my first class wanted to add a room onto her house and do some remodeling. She had meditated for two years, but still didn't have the room. After attending the class for two sessions and employing the techniques, a friend and her husband were visiting and the husband said he would remodel and add a room onto her house for only $200. A professional at remodeling, he ended up completing a $5000 job for the $200 she could well afford.
- A friend of mine who took the class wanted to be self-employed in a home business with flexible hours. She had worked for companies in their sales department for years and was tired of the 9 to 5 schedule. She developed a vacuum by setting up an office in her home. Within 3 weeks, she called me to say that she had quit her desk job and had her own home business with flexible hours.

Please see www.conniedomino.com for many more recent success stories and case studies!

Appendix B – Feeling Words Lists

Positive Feelings

Intense

loved, adored, idolized, alive, wanted, lustful, worthy, respected, empathy, awed, enthusiastic, zealous, courageous

Strong

enchanted, ardor, infatuated, tender, vibrant, independent, capable, happy, proud, gratified, worthy, sympathetic, important, concerned, appreciated, consoled, delighted, eager, optimistic, joyful, courage, hopeful, valiant, brave, brilliant

Moderate

liked, cared for, esteemed, affectionate, fond, excited, patient, strong, inspired, anticipating, amused, yearning, popular, peaceful, appealing, determined, pleased, excited, jolly, relieved, glad, adventurous, peaceful, intelligent

Mild

friendly, regarded, benevolent, wide awake, at-ease, relaxed, comfortable, content, keen, amazed, alert, sure, attractive, approved, untroubled, graceful, turned on, warm, amused, daring, comfortable, smart, interested

Negative Feelings

Mild

unpopular, listless, moody, lethargic, gloomy, dismal, discontented, tired, indifferent, unsure, impatient, dependent, unimportant, regretful, bashful, puzzled, self-conscious, edgy, upset, reluctant, timid, mixed-up, sullen

Appendix B - Feeling Words Lists

Moderate

suspicious, envious, enmity, aversion, dejected, unhappy, bored, forlorn, disappointed, wearied, inadequate, ineffectual, helpless, resigned, apathetic, shy, uncomfortable, baffled, confused, nervous, tempted, tense, worried, perplexed, troubled, disdainful, contemptuous, alarmed, annoyed, provoked

Strong

disgusted, resentful, bitter, detested, fed-up, frustrated, sad, depressed, sick, dissatisfied, fatigued, worn-out, useless, weak, hopeless, forlorn, rejected, guilty, embarrassed, inhibited, bewildered, frightened, anxious, dismayed, apprehensive, disturbed, antagonistic, vengeful, indignant, mad, torn

Intense

hate, unloved, abhor, despised, angry, hurt, miserable, pain, lonely, cynical, worthless, impotent, futile, accursed, abandoned, estranged, degraded, humiliated, shocked, panicky, trapped, horrified, afraid, scared, terrified, threatened, infuriated, furious, exhausted

Feelings document used with permission of innercom. Communicating Inner Calm. Webmaster David M. Hazen, located in Eugene, Oregon, USA, 2003[2]

http://www.cyberis.net/~innercom/TxDocs/feelingwordsalt.html

Appendix C – Sample Global Affirmations

Remember that globally written affirmations do not take the place of the very specifically written, measurable and behavioral (with a target date) affirmations written for our desired goal. However, they can be used in support of your desired goal objective. They can also be used to bust up energy blocks/boulders. I have placed these global affirmations under the four main desire categories. Money and Career are combined.

Love and Relationships

- I love unconditionally and by doing so, unconditional love is automatically returned to me.
- I am a magnet for positive, loving experiences.
- I know clearly who I am and what I want in my personal relationships.
- I attract powerfully positive and healthy people into my life.
- Growth and change in my intimate love relationships is always directed toward good.
- I am wise, honest, thoughtful, and healthy in my love relationships, and others treat me the same.
- I am in a fulfilling relationship with my ideal partner.
- All of my desires in my relationships are fulfilled.
- Because I am completely confident in my health, honesty, and inner wisdom, I invest in personal relationships knowing deeply that I can deal with anything I may need to.
- I am capable of an open, honest, loving, and fulfilling relationship.
- Love comes to me easily and effortlessly.
- I make valuable contributions in my relationships daily.
- I know only love, and know that there is no need to be afraid in any of my relationships.
- I am special and deserve love.

Appendix C - Sample Global Affirmations

Money and Career

- I now accept abundance into my life, as I am a deserving, divine being, and always have been. God is my unfailing supply, and large sums of money come to me.
- I now manifest my dreams in the form of prosperity and abundance.
- I create a positive, joyful, and abundant life.
- I am a magnet for divine abundance in the form of money, health, and happiness.
- I am financially secure and successful.
- I have plenty of time and money.
- I am open to receive the abundance of the Universe.
- I am constantly adding to my income.
- I am the embodiment of abundance, which manifests in my life as perfect health, wealth, and constant happiness.
- I am in a successful career.
- I am in the perfect career, which manifests $____ or more annually.
- I am now acting upon my life purpose with joy and passion.
- I am certain that my path is always perfect for me.
- I am always successful and the Universe sees only the perfection in everything, and I choose to see it too.

Health and Healing

- Just because I walk this earth, I am a worthwhile child of God.
- I embrace peace and healing.
- Everyday, in every way, I am getting better and better!
- I feel good about myself and I love myself.
- I am connected to the Divine, and I am now whole and perfect.
- I now begin the process of well-being and good health by loving my past, present, and future selves.
- I create positive energy in my life by placing love, light, and laughter around me.

Develop Irresistible Attraction

- I choose love, joy, peace, and vibrant health for myself, humanity, and the Earth.
- I am the embodiment of perfect health at all times.
- I choose to accept the healing path that resonates with me.
- I am in the flow of Divine love, which ensures joy, peace, love, health, and happiness at all levels of my existence.
- I have the power to control my health.
- I am in control of my health and wellness.
- I have abundant energy, vitality and well-being.
- I love and care for my body, and it cares for me.

Remember, only use Global Affirmations for support in addition to your specific measurable goal affirmations; they are not to replace them. Each desired goal should have a specific measurable affirmation with a goal date listed.

Appendix D – The Law of Attraction Recommended Starter Reading List

Ponder, Catherine, *The Dynamic Laws of Prosperity* (DeVorss Publications, 1996).

This is the primer for our LOA class and a must read. Catherine Ponder is a Unity Minister. In her easy to read and entertaining book, she covers the Law of Attraction, The Vacuum Law of Prosperity, the Law of Forgiveness, and more. She has written many affirmations throughout the book that you can use. This is a good book to learn how to write your own affirmations as well.

> *"There are also higher mental and spiritual laws than those usually used on the physical plane of life. Jesus knew and used them constantly. These higher mental and spiritual laws are so powerful that they can be used to multiply, neutralize, or even reverse natural laws! It is when these higher mental and spirituals laws are used by the mind of man, that they often produce results that seem miraculous on the physical plane." (6).*

Grabhorn, Lynn, *Excuse Me Your Life is Waiting* (Hampton Roads Publishing Co., Inc., 2001).

Lynn Grabhorn, in her easy to read and entertaining book, explains how universal energy works and how we can use energy to help ourselves and others. She also has a companion *Playbook* that will carry the reader through exercises that will increase their understanding of their great potential to vibrate high and manifest their dreams into reality. My LOA students have also enjoyed her audio tapes.

Develop Irresistible Attraction

"When you finally understand that you can generate that which you have been desperately looking for outside yourself, you become the master of your life." (256).

Giovanni, Katharine, *God, Is That You?* (New Road Publishing, 2002).

In her inspirational book, author and speaker Katharine Giovanni shows you how to have an actual conversation with God. Uplifting and anecdotal in nature, this nondenominational guide teaches people how to have a two-way conversation with God by offering examples of how to listen to God's voice and receive answers back in real words and sentences. It challenges people to listen to the voice of God in their everyday lives and to understand that they can hold conversations with God on a daily basis.

Outlining a simple, easy-to-learn technique, this book stresses that anyone can listen to God – He doesn't just talk to religious leaders like Cardinals, Rabbis, and Ministers. For those seeking clear, understandable answers or the spiritually curious, this book offers real-world examples of how to have a more personal relationship with God.

"This is your golden moment of realization. The hope of a better way. The hope of better things yet to come. The realization that God actually speaks and exists. He really is here, and he loves you." (2).

Butterworth, Eric, *Discover the Power Within You* (San Francisco: Harper Collins Publishers, 1989).

Eric Butterworth, a Unity minister, explains how to awaken to the powerful spiritual being you really are. He relates this information to the Bible. You will really enjoy the amazing insights you will gain from reading this book.

"When we know the Truth of this great spiritual potential within us which Jesus called the Kingdom of God within, we are free to be-

come our unlimited self, free to do unlimited things. We see things in a different light, we react to a different set of principles, we draw upon a higher potential, a potential that has always been within us, which has always really been us." (24).

Bach, Richard, *Illusions: The Adventures of a Reluctant Messiah* (Dell/ Eleanor Friede Book, 1977).

The author of *Jonathan Livingston Seagull*, Richard Bach weaves a dynamic and spiritually insightful tale of what it would be like for the Messiah to come to Earth today. This cleverly written book, will increase your awareness of what Jesus was really all about and will shed light on your own divinity. It is an easy read and the concepts just flow.

"Learning is finding out what you already know. Doing is demonstrating that you know it. Teaching is reminding others that they know just as well as you. You are all learners, doers, teachers." (58).

Redfield, James, *The Celestine Vision* (Warner Books, 1997).

James Redfield, author of many books, including *The Celestine Prophecy* and *The Tenth Insight,* does an excellent job of describing the historical and scientific background of the spiritual awakening being experienced by so many people today. He examines one hundred years in physics, psychology and religion to demonstrate an amazing synthesis of Eastern and Western thought. He then details how we can apply understanding of this new spiritual awareness to make our lives and our world a better place.

"Before we go out of the house, we must find that space, that spiritual posture, in which we live what we know. The power of faith is real. Every thought is a prayer, and if the vision of the new spiritual awareness resides in the back of our minds every day, every minute,

*as we interact in the world, the magic of synchronicity will acceler-
ate for everyone, and the destiny we intuit in our hearts will become
a reality." (233-234).*

**Ban Breathnach, Sarah, *Simple Abundance: A Daybook of Comfort and
Joy* (Warner Books, 1995).**

This wonderfully written, delightful book takes the reader through a year of
learning and living a simple abundant and authentic life. I have read it at least
three times and still have epiphanies and revelations every time. It's a wonderful gift book for people who are just beginning their spiritual journey. It is
equally enjoyable for those that have been journeying for years. It's a book
that will be welcomed by most any woman of any personal belief system.
Sarah has also written a number of companion books, including *A Man's
Journey to Simple Abundance.*

*"Simple Abundance evolved from creating a manageable lifestyle
into living in a state of grace, I began to barely recognize the woman
I once was. Simple Abundance has enabled me to encounter everyday epiphanies, find the Sacred in the ordinary, the Mystical in the
mundane, fully enter into the sacrament of the present moment. Simple
Abundance has reminded me what to do with a few loaves and fishes
and has shown me how to spin straw into gold. Simple Abundance
has given me the transcendent awareness that an authentic life is the
most personal form of worship. Everyday life has become my prayer.
Writing Simple Abundance has brought me to the awareness that the
reason I was so unhappy, frustrated, resentful, envious and angry
was because I wasn't living the Real life for which I was created. An
authentic life." (Foreword).*

In addition, to those on this list, I recommend any of the books listed in my
Notes. I have read these books, and know they contain great wisdom. Most
of these authors have other excellent books available as well.

Notes

Epigraph

1. Henry David Thoreau quoted in Butterworth, Eric, *The Universe Is Calling: Opening to the Divine Through Prayer* (San Francisco: Harper Collins Publishers, 1993), 31.

2. Oprah, *O Magazine*. Quote found on www.quotationspage.com, 2004.

Chapter 1

1. Hill, Napoleon, *Think and Grow Rich* (New York: Facwett Books, 1960), 14.

2. Vecchione, Patrice, *Writing and the Spiritual Life* (Contemporary Books, 2001), 96.

3. Pierre Teilhard De Chardin quoted in Robinson, Lynn A.*, Divine Intuition: Your Guide to Creating a Life You Love* (London: Dorling Kindersley, 2001), 155.

4. Lama, Dalai, and Howard C. Cutler, *The Art of Happiness* (New York Riverbead Books, 1998), 13.

5. Redfield, James, *The Celestine Vision* (Warner Books, 1997), 4.

6. James Allen as quoted in Robinson, Lynn A.*, Divine Intuition: Your Guide to Creating a Life You Love* (London: Dorling Kindersley, 2001), 140.

7. Dossey, Larry, *Healing Words: The Power of Prayer and the Practice of Medicine* (San Francisco: Harper Collins, 1993), 180.

8. Dossey, Larry, *Healing Words: The Power of Prayer and the Practice of Medicine* (San Francisco: Harper Collins, 1993), 190.

9. Clark, Ronald, W., *Einstein: The Life and Times* (New York: Avon, 1984), 649.

Chapter 2

1. Vanzant, Iyanla, *One Day My Soul Just Opened Up* (Simon and Schuster, 1998), 78.

2. Walsch, Neale Donald, *Relationships: Applications to Living* (Hampton Roads Publishing, Inc., 1999), 39.

3. Vecchione, Patrice, *Writing and the Spiritual Life* (Contemporary Books, 2001), 98.

Chapter 3

1. Oprah, *O Magazine.* Quote found on www.quotationspage.com, 2004.

2. Hart, Louise, *The Winning Family: Increasing Self-Esteem In Your Children and Yourself* (Lifeskills Press, 1990), 114.

3. McGraw, Phillip C., *Self Matters: Creating Your Life from the Inside Out* (Free Press/Simon and Schuster, Inc., 2001), 205.

4. Zukav, Gary, *Thoughts from the Seat of the Soul* (New York: Simon and Schuster, Inc., 1994), 197.

Notes

5. Vanzant, Iyanla, *One Day My Soul Just Opened Up* (Simon and Schuster, 1998), 40.

6. Zukav, Gary, *Thoughts from the Seat of the Soul* (New York: Simon and Schuster, Inc., 1994), 32.

7. Marianne Williamson as quoted in Robinson, Lynn A*., Divine Intuition: Your Guide to Creating a Life You Love* (London: Dorling Kindersley, 2001), 118.

8. Zukav, Gary, *Thoughts from the Seat of the Soul* (New York: Simon and Schuster, Inc., 1994), 22.

9. Hart, Louise, *The Winning Family: Increasing Self-Esteem In Your Children and Yourself* (Lifeskills Press, 1990), 115.

Chapter 4

1. Rainer Maria Rilke as quoted in Fox, Matthew, *Original Blessing (Sante Fe, NM: Bear and Company Publishing, 1983), 201.

2. Dyer, Wayne, W., *There is a Spiritual Solution to Every Problem* (Harper Collins Publishers, 2001), 190.

Chapter 6

1. Hubbard, Elbert, *The Philosophy of Elbert Hubbard* (The Roycrofters, 1916), 126.

Chapter 7

1. Johnson, Spencer, *Who Moved My Cheese?* (GP Putnam and Sons, 1998), 27.

2. Henry Ford as quoted in Hart, Louise, *The Winning Family: Increasing Self-Esteem In Your Children and Yourself* (Lifeskills Press, 1990), 109.

3. Meister Eckhart as quoted in Hart, Louise, *The Winning Family: Increasing Self-Esteem In Your Children and Yourself* (Lifeskills Press, 1990), 41.

4. Grabhorn, Lynn, *Excuse Me Your Life Is Waiting* (Hampton Roads Publishing Co., Inc., 2001), 13.

5. Zukav, Gary, *Thoughts from the Seat of the Soul* (New York: Simon and Schuster, Inc., 1994), 200.

6. Johnson, Spencer, *Who Moved My Cheese?* (GP Putnam and Sons, 1998), 64.

7. Gannon, Kenny, *Blocks:* Acting Class Follow Up Personal Email, 7-22-02.

Chapter 8

1. Angela Monet as quoted in Berg, Yehuda, *The Power of the Kabbalah* (Jodere Group, Inc., 2001) , xxv.

2. Ponder, Catherine, *The Dynamic Laws of Prosperity* (Devorss Publications, 1996), 41-42.

3. Angelou, Maya, *Wouldn't Take Nothing for My Journey Now* (New York: Bantam Books, 1993), 139.

Chapter 9

1. Vanzant, Iyanla, *One Day My Soul Just Opened Up* (Simon and Schuster, 1998), 168.

Notes

2. Zukav, Gary, *Thoughts from the Seat of the Soul* (New York: Simon and Schuster, Inc., 1994), 191.

3. Hart, Louise, *The Winning Family: Increasing Self-Esteem In Your Children and Yourself* (Lifeskills Press, 1990), 39.

4. Eric Holfer as quoted in Hart, Louise, *The Winning Family: Increasing Self-Esteem In Your Children and Yourself* (Lifeskills Press, 1990), 17.

5. Ponder, Catherine, *The Dynamic Laws of Prosperity* (Devorss Publications, 1996), 44.

Chapter 10

1. Berg, Yehuda, *The Power of the Kabbalah* (Jodere Group, Inc., 2001), 224.

2. Johnson, Spencer, *Who Moved My Cheese?* (GP Putnam and Sons, 1998), 58.

Chapter 12

1. Redfield, James, *The Celestine Vision* (Warner Books, 1997), 11.

Chapter 13

1. Tipping, Colin C., *Radical Forgiveness: Making Room for the Miracle*, 2nd. Edition (Global 13 Publications, 2002), 99.

192

Develop Irresistible Attraction

Chapter 14

1. Rubin, Ron and Stuart Avery Gold, *Success @ Life: A Zentrepreneur's Guide How to Catch and Live Your Dream* (NY: Newmarket Press, 2001), 43.

2. Grabhorn, Lynn, *Excuse Me Your Life Is Waiting* (Hampton Roads Publishing Co., Inc., 2001), 13.

Chapter 15

1. Vecchione, Patrice, *Writing and the Spiritual Life* (Contemporary Books, 2001), 96.

2. Dyer, Wayne, W., *There is a Spiritual Solution to Every Problem* (Harper Collins Publishers, 2001), xvi.

3. Morris, Mike, "I Shop Therefore I Think" (*The News and Observer*, August 14, 2003), IE.

4. Siegel, Bernie S., *Love, Medicine and Miracles* (Harper Perennial, 1986), 183.

5. Siegel, Bernie S., *Love, Medicine and Miracles* (Harper Perennial, 1986), 183.

6. Siegel, Bernie S., *Love, Medicine and Miracles* (Harper Perennial, 1986), 144.

7. Suzanne Sugarbaker as quoted in Browne, Jill Conner, *The Sweet Potato Queens' Book of Love* (Three Rivers Press, 1999), 4.

Notes

Chapter 16

1. Walsch, Neale Donald, *Relationships: Applications to Living* (Hampton Roads Publishing, Inc., 1999), 17.

2. Albert Clarke as quoted in Robinson, Lynn A.*, Divine Intuition: Your Guide to Creating a Life You Love* (London: Dorling Kindersley, 2001), 114.

3. Ban Breathnach, Sarah, *Simple Abundance: A Daybook of Comfort and Joy* (Time Warner, 1995), Jan. 14.

4. Hay, Louise, *You Can Heal Your Life* (Carson CA: Haye House, Inc., 1987), 99.

5. McWilliams, Peter, *Come with Me and be My Life: The Complete Romantic Poetry of Peter McWilliams* (Prelude Press, 2000), 244.

6. Butterworth, Eric, *The Power Is Within You* (San Francisco: Harper Collins Publishers, 1989), 40.

Chapter 17

1. Orman, Suze, *The 9 Steps to Financial Freedom* (New York: Crown Publishers, Inc., 1997), 7.

Chapter 19

1. McWilliams, Peter, *Come with Me and be My Life: The Complete Romantic Poetry of Peter McWilliams* (Prelude Press, 2000), 11.

2. Walsch, Neale Donald, *Relationships: Applications to Living* (Hampton Roads Publishing, Inc., 1999), 17.

3. Hart, Louise, *The Winning Family: Increasing Self-Esteem In Your Children and Yourself* (Lifeskills Press, 1990), 161.

4. Lao Tzu as quoted in Hart, Louise, *The Winning Family: Increasing Self-Esteem In Your Children and Yourself* (Lifeskills Press, 1990), 61.

5. Shain, Merle, *When Lovers are Friends* (Bantum Books, 1978), 85.

6.   McWilliams, Peter, *Come with Me and be My Life: The Complete Romantic Poetry of Peter McWilliams* (Prelude Press, 2000), 10.

7. Giovanni, Katharine, *God Is That You?* (New Road Publishing, 2002), 10.

8. Giovanni, Katharine, *God Is That You?* (New Road Publishing, 2002), 78.

9. Zukav, Gary, *Thoughts from the Seat of the Soul* (New York: Simon and Schuster, Inc., 1994), 162.

Chapter 20

1. Nerburn, Kent, *Simple Truths: Gentle Guidance on the Big Issues in Life* (NY: Barnes and Noble Books, 1996), 22.

Chapter 21

1. Hawkins, David R., *Power vs. Force: The Hidden Determinants of Human Behavior* (Hay House, Inc., 2002), 219.

Notes

2. Johnson, Benn, *American South: Celebrate Southerness, Ya'll* (Birmingham Printing and Publishing, Inc., 2002), Benn on Religion.

Chapter 22

1. Hazen, David, *Feelings Word List*, www.cyberis.net/~innercom/TxDocs/feelingwordsalt.html, 2003.

For Book Study Groups and Book Clubs

I have designed a complimentary book study guide for those who would like to work through the material and exercises with others. For book clubs that are already formed, you may find the study guide questions helpful. For those who would like to form a book study group in their neighborhood, civic group, lunch bunch at work, church or other religious organization, etc. the guide includes complete information on how to form one or more groups.

The free downloadable book study guide is available from my website at www.conniedomino.com. If you wish to purchase books in bulk for your group(s), please email publisher@ LOAQuantumGrowth.com.

Quick Order Form

Fax Orders: 919-571-8769

Telephone Orders: 919-368-8041

Email Orders: publisher@LOAQuantumGrowth.com

Postal Orders: LOA Quantum Growth LLC, 7805 Tylerton Drive, Raleigh, NC 27613

Please send me _____ copies of your book ***Develop Irresistible Attraction*** by Connie Domino. I am including the cover price of $14.95 per book plus the shipping charges as described below. I understand that I may return the book for a full refund (minus postage) for any reason. Contact us for bulk order rates (919-368-8041).

Name: _____

Address: _____

City: _____ State: _____ Zip Code: _____

Country: _____

Telephone Number: ( ) _____

Email Address: _____

SALES TAX: Please add 7% for books shipped to North Carolina Addresses.

SHIPPING: In the United States please add $4.00 for the first book and $2.00 for each additional book. For international orders please add $9.00 for the first book and $5.00 for each additional book.

PAYMENT: Please circle ONE

Personal Check   *Visa*   *MasterCard*   *Discover*

Credit Card Number: _____

Expiration Date: _____

Name on Card: _____

Signature: _____

Develop Irresistible Attraction

Connie Domino, BSN, MPH, RN

Author, Speaker, Consultant

Connie is an author, trainer, speaker, life and business coach, public health educator and registered nurse. She has 20 years experience in business, health promotion and wellness education. Connie owns a successful consulting business providing education, training, grant writing and program coordination for agencies, organizations, and businesses. She provides education and training programs on a variety of topics for women, teachers, parents, youth and other professionals.

Connie also has training and experience as a support group facilitator, educational counselor, and motivational speaker. She received her B.S. in Nursing from Florida State University and a Master of Public Health from the University of North Carolina at Chapel Hill. Connie currently resides in North Carolina with her husband and two children.

For more information about books, tapes, CDs, newsletters, personal or organizational coaching and consultation, conference calls, speaking and training engagements, please contact LOA Quantum Growth LLC at: www.ConnieDomino.com.